Gardeners' World magazine

First Time
Veg Grower

Gardeners' World magazine

First Time Veg Grower

Author
Martyn Cox

BOOKS

Contents

Introduction

Nothing compares to home-grown vegetables. Shelling pods, unearthing roots or picking fruit when they are perfectly ripe means they will taste far superior to anything you'll buy from the shops.

But the grow-your-own renaissance is not just about flavour; many want to raise crops in their gardens to save money on their weekly shopping bills or to produce ingredients for the table that they know haven't been touched with pesticides or artificial fertilizers. Some do it so they have access to vegetables that aren't commonly available without visiting a specialist food market, while a good proportion grow their own food because of the satisfaction they get from tucking into a meal that includes ingredients they started off from seed.

Whatever your reason to grow your own, there's never been a better time to start. Seed companies are releasing more and more tempting varieties to satisfy the vegetable growing demand, including many that are suitable for the tiniest of spaces – these compact crops can be grown

successfully in pots, meaning anyone, whatever size of garden they have, can enjoy growing their own.

However, if the last crop you grew was a batch of cress on cotton wool while at secondary school, you might feel a little bewildered. Perhaps you don't know where to start and are asking yourself: What should I grow? Where should I grow it? How can I look after the plants to ensure they don't succumb to pests and diseases? If this sounds like you, don't despair. This book will guide you through the basics and ensure that your first season of growing your own vegetables is a resounding success.

Martyn Cox

How to get started

There's nothing more exciting than deciding to grow your own vegetables for the first time and you'll naturally be impatient to get going as soon as possible. But before spending a fortune on a 'shop 'til you drop' outing at your local garden centre or nursery, where you'll be tempted to snap up every plant or packet of seeds that takes your fancy, take a deep breath, pause for a moment and spend a little time planning exactly what you would like to grow.

Many newbie veg growers make the mistake of growing crops that they either don't have the space for, that require more time and effort than they can afford to give, or that aren't suited to the location they intend to grow them in – whether it's on an allotment, in a back garden or on a balcony attached to a flat.

By picking varieties that suit your lifestyle and your garden, you'll ensure that your vegetables thrive, rather than limp along, and you'll enjoy nurturing your crops from plot to plate, rather than being put off for life. If you derive pleasure from raising your vegetables you'll be ready and willing to do it all again the following year, rather than being jaded by the whole experience because it was all rather a tiresome chore.

How much space do you have?

If you've got a country house, surrounded by a few rolling acres, the only restriction on what you can grow is how much time you can dedicate to looking after the plants. However, if you're strapped for space you need to think a little more carefully about what to grow.

Many vegetables billow out sideways, spread rapidly or shoot upwards as if someone has put a rocket under them. In a diminutive garden these plants can rob you of precious space, making what was already a tiny plot appear even smaller. So, even though you love to eat sweetcorn, globe artichokes, asparagus, Brussels sprouts or another crop that grows into a big beast, give them a wide berth. These vegetables are best kept for the allotment, kitchen garden or dedicated vegetable patch, rather than a tiny back garden where you will end up being unable to grow anything else.

Another reason not to take up precious space with these large plants is the amount of time they take from sowing to harvesting – they are real plodders. Aside from the perennials, that will be in the ground all year round, many crops that are grown as annuals each year need to be in-situ for six months or more – so by the time you come to pick the vegetables you'll be fed up with the sight of it. A far better use of limited space is to fill it with more compact crops or with a fast-growing vegetable that can be harvested several weeks after sowing. Once picked, it can then be replaced with another vegetable, making whatever gap you are using really earn its keep.

If you have a very small garden, you need to be even more realistic. If you only have room for a window box, you can forget about growing cordon tomatoes, runner beans or potatoes. Think small and pick tumbling tomatoes, mixed salad leaves, radishes, spring onions or a compact, dwarf French bean.

How much time do you have?

When you take that first step and decide to grow your own vegetables you'll probably find that you get swept along on a huge tide of enthusiasm that will result in you wanting to grow everything you possibly can. Well, without wanting to sound too much like a curmudgeon, please take it easy to

Even a hanging basket can support a number of crops.

begin with or you might end up putting yourself off growing vegetables for life.

You have to be realistic about how much time you have to spend looking after your plants, and this in turn will influence where and what you grow. If you can only put aside a few minutes each week, there's no point in taking on an allotment, filling it with plants and then finding out that you simply don't have the free time to put in the necessary hours. In these circumstances the trip to the allotment soon becomes a chore and you're likely to be put off going, with the inevitable result of being ticked off by the

Choose crops carefully

The amount of free time you have can impact on what plants you grow. For example, tomatoes, cucumbers, peppers, aubergines and some beans need a lot of tender, loving care during their growth or you will end up with a poor crop; while potatoes, carrots, beetroot and many salads need less attention to produce a bumper harvest.

allotment secretary because you've allowed the plot to become a weed-filled mess.

If you lead a busy life, start small and keep things easily manageable and close to home. Try growing a few vegetables in pots, or in a dedicated patch where you can keep an eye on them easily from the house and give them attention when they need it. If this still sounds like too much of a commitment, but you are determined to grow your own, make life easier by cutting down on some tasks. Simple things can help, such as using mulches around plants to prevent weeds from growing or installing an automatic irrigation system connected to a timer so you won't need to make regular trips with the watering can (*see page 177*).

Far left **Compact vegetables in a pot.**
Left **Colourful chard looks and tastes good.**

Site, situation and soil

Vegetables can be grown in just about every type of garden, but the amount of sunshine it receives and the type of soil you have can play in a big part in what you can grow. Once you've learned more about your plot you can improve your soil if necessary, or even prepare a seed bed to get young plants growing vigorously from the start.

Aspect

Most vegetables will do best in a sunny, sheltered position, where the combination of heat, light and protection from strong winds will encourage them to grow vigorously and allow the crops to ripen to perfection. However, many people who have small gardens in towns and cities often find that their space is partially shaded by neighbouring buildings or nearby trees.

As a general rule, vegetables that are grown for their roots and fruit need the sunniest spots and will simply sulk if you deprive them of light. But don't be put off if you have far from perfect growing conditions such as these. Although yields are going to be lower in a garden that is shaded, there are still crops, such as beetroot, that you can grow.

Growing your own beetroot

1 Sowing the seeds
Make a straight, shallow trench 2cm deep and sow the seeds in pairs thinly along the bottom.

2 Covering up
Cover the seeds carefully with the excavated soil.

3 Firming down
Firm the soil down gently with your hand to ensure the seeds make good contact with the soil.

4 Thinning out your crop
When seedlings are 2cm tall, remove the weakest of each pair to give them plenty of space to grow.

Plants that are grown for their leaves or stems, or that grow at a blistering pace, will do fine in partial shade, although they won't be happy if grown in full shade. Among the other plants to try in conditions like this are lettuce, radish, Swiss chard and blends of mixed salad leaves. Although they are a bit slower to get going when grown in the shade, they are so fast growing that they will still provide you with a worthwhile crop when there's little light.

Know your soil

You can get away with growing vegetables in just about any kind of soil, but they will do best in fertile soil that has an open texture, which allows excess water to drain away, and that contains a good amount of organic matter, which will help to hold on to moisture and prevent crops drying out quickly when water is scarce.

Although novice vegetable growers may think soil is just, well, soil, there are actually several different types out there. The sort of soil you possess can have an impact on what vegetables you can grow, and how productive they will be. Soils vary a lot depending on where in the country you are. The three most common types of soil are clay, sandy and silty; other soils you may find are peaty and chalk.

You can find out what kind of soil you have in a very rough and ready way. Simply dig up a handful of weed-free earth and try to roll it into a ball.

If the soil is sticky and can be moulded into a ball it's a loamy clay soil; a heavy clay soil is likely to be even more malleable and can be smoothed out quite thinly without falling apart. Clay soils are fairly fertile, but a heavy clay can become waterlogged in winter and will dry rock-solid in summer. These soils can be improved by digging in plenty of well-rotted manure along with a few handfuls of grit, which will open up the soil and improve the drainage while also enabling it to hold onto moisture more effectively in summer. This is essential to prevent the clay from turning into a material resembling concrete. Alternatively, if this sounds like hard work, forget about trying to tame a particularly heavy clay soil and grow your veg in raised beds filled with good-quality compost instead.

If the soil feels fairly gritty and doesn't hold together when you try to form it into a ball, you have sandy soil. This tends to be well drained, which will prevent waterlogging in winter, but it will mean you need to water crops frequently over summer to prevent them becoming thirsty. You may also need to feed regularly as nutrients will be flushed away

Chalky soils can often be very stony.

Clay soil sticks together when rolled in the hands.

Peaty soils are dark and rich in colour.

through the soil quickly. On the positive side, they are much lighter and easier to cultivate than clay soils.

Sandy soils benefit from having well-rotted manure or garden compost dug in. This bulks up the soil and enables it to hold onto nutrients and water more effectively, enabling the roots of plants to get what they need. A good idea is to mulch damp soil in spring – this will help it to retain moisture by reducing surface evaporation (*see p195*).

Soil that feels silky when it is rubbed between hands, and that sticks together, is described as silty. These are generally fertile soils that hold onto moisture, but compact easily when walked on, causing problems with drainage. Digging in well-rotted manure or compost will help improve the soil's structure and prevent it from compacting too easily.

Chalky soils are very stony and often light in colour. They drain freely, which can result in the soil becoming very dry. Its ability to hold on to moisture can be improved by adding compost or well-rotted manure, followed by mulching to prevent moisture loss. Peaty soils are dark in colour and very fertile. They hold on to moisture, but need working well to improve drainage.

Soil acidity

You will often hear experienced gardeners talk about soil acidity or pH values and wonder what on earth they are talking about. Very simply, soil acidity is recorded on a pH scale of 1 to 14. A pH of 7 indicates that the soil is neutral; scale points above this are alkaline and anything beneath signals that the soil is acidic.

pH for produce

A pH of 6.5–7 is considered to be ideal for most vegetables, and this is what is most commonly found in gardens. However, if yours is more acidic or alkaline it doesn't mean you can't grow anything – soils that are alkaline suit cabbages and other brassica crops, while acidic soils are ideal for plants like rhubarb or potatoes.

It is very easy to establish the pH level of your soil. There are various testing devices available. Those that are cheap and cheerful will give you a rough indication of the pH level, while hi-tech gadgets are more expensive but will give you a more accurate reading.

The most common soil-testing kits consist of a test tube that contains a powdered chemical. After popping in some of your soil, you add water and give it a shake. As it settles the colour of the contents can be measured against a chart

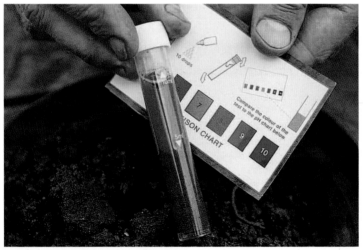

A simple soil test will reveal the acidity of your soil.

to give the pH. The more advanced devices have probes that can be pushed into the soil to give a reading on a meter – these are ideal if you have a large plot of land as the pH of the soil can change within the same location and you may want to test a few different areas. However, if you only have a small plot you should find that a test-tube kit will work perfectly well for you.

Most gardeners will find that vegetables are generally quite tolerant of their soils; it's only when there are extremes of acidity or alkalinity that there are problems. The pH level of acid soils can be raised by spreading lime over the soil, making it more neutral. Very alkaline soils are harder to alter, but digging in leaf mould made from pine needles or shredded pine bark will help.

Removing weeds

If a would-be vegetable garden only has a few annual or perennial weeds they can be easily dealt with when you prepare the soil by digging. If the ground has been neglected for some time and is infested with weeds, however it will need clearing before you can plunge in a spade.

Whatever you do, do not be tempted to hire a mechanical cultivator to turn over weed-infested land. Although this will result in soil that you can plant into immediately, you will end up creating years of problems for yourself. Brambles, couch grass, bindweed and other pernicious weeds have underground roots that, when broken up, have the ability to re-grow. If you chop these up with a cultivator you could potentially spread the problem throughout the plot and be forever trying to remove the weeds as they grow up through your vegetables.

So how can you banish weeds effectively? Well, this depends on whether you are prepared to use chemical herbicides. The quickest way of dealing with them, and avoiding lots of hard work, is to spray the ground with a weedkiller containing glyphosate. Known as a systemic herbicide, it enters the leaves and travels down to the roots, killing the plant completely within seven days or so. After this, you can start to prepare the soil – the chemical does not reside in the soil and harm anything you plant into it.

While this method is ideal for most weeds, some need tougher treatment. If you have taken on an abandoned allotment you may find that it is smothered in brambles. The best approach is to first reduce the tangle of growth above

Right **Remove weeds before they set seed.**
Far right **Pest infestations may require control with pesticides.**

the ground with a brush cutter, then spray the battered stumps with a more powerful formula of glyphosate, such as those found in the rootkillers or herbicides that are recommended for killing Japanese knotweed. Alternatively, if a plot only has a few patches of brambles, use a fork to prise the roots from the soil, making sure you remove every last bit.

While the use of herbicides will quickly give you a piece of ground that is ready for cultivation, they are, however, chemicals. If you prefer an organic approach to growing your own you need to try other methods of weed control.

Persistent digging and hoeing can rid land of many invasive weeds, but it might take a couple of years. If you decide on digging, fork out as much of the root system as possible when cultivating the soil in autumn and winter. In spring, dig out any new shoots as they appear.

If you have a large area of soil that is infested with perennial weeds, consider digging them out from part of it and covering the rest in plastic, landscape material or even a piece of old carpet. This will prevent new weeds from germinating and deprive those already in the ground of much-needed light, which will weaken and eventually kill them.

Preparing your soil

Before you can start growing vegetables in the ground, you need to put aside some time to prepare it; essentially this means removing weeds, digging over the soil and fertilizing to give any plants you grow a boost.

If possible, the best time to tackle new vegetable beds is in the autumn. Digging at this time helps to reveal soil-borne pests to hungry birds, while exposing heavy clods to frost helps break them down, making it perfect for sowing or planting in a few months' time.

Work plenty of well-rotted manure into your soil when digging.

There are three main ways of cultivating the soil. Simple digging is sufficient in most gardens, especially if you need to work around plants. All you have to do is remove a clod, and turn it over, chopping it up a bit with your spade. If you have very stony or heavy clay soil, you may find this easier to do with a garden fork.

On large areas it is best to single dig. To do this, start at one end of the area and excavate a trench to the depth of the spade's blade (this measurement is known by gardeners

as a spit), then transport the soil to the other end of the plot with a wheelbarrow. Now spread some well-rotted farmyard manure or garden compost in the base of the trench and dig out another, dropping the soil into the first one. Carry on like this until you reach the end of the plot, removing perennial weeds and burying annuals. Fill the final trench with the soil removed from the first trench.

If you take on a really weed-infested plot, which hasn't been cultivated for years, roll up your sleeves and try a spot of double digging. With this method, soil is cultivated to the depth of two spits by first removing a trench with a spade and then forking over the bottom of the trench to the depth of the tines of the fork.

A garden fork makes light work of clay soil.

Making a seed bed

After digging the ground, you need to further cultivate the top layer of soil before you sow seeds or introduce plants – the ideal texture should resemble fine breadcrumbs. The best time to do this is in spring, working on ground that was dug in autumn and exposed to the elements over winter, rather than freshly dug soil that will require a lot more elbow grease to prepare.

Start by working methodically across your plot with a fork, using the tool to break down any large clods. To do this you'll have to use a combination of stabbing and hitting the soil with the tines. After you've worked over the entire area, roughly level the soil with the fork. There's no need to be too precise at this stage.

Next, use a rake to draw soil into any hollows or to even out mounds. Rake the soil backwards and forwards in one direction until the clods have all gone and the soil has a fine, even finish. Then rake in another direction, 90 degrees to the first. Lastly, rake the soil to leave a flat and even surface, removing any stones you unearth. This part of preparing the bed does require effort, but the end result of a clean and even sheet of soil is incredibly rewarding and means your seeds and plants will establish quickly.

Rake soil until it resembles the texture of breadcrumbs.

Seeds, plugs or plants?

There's nothing more satisfying than serving up a dish containing vegetables you started off from seed. The care and attention you have given the plant over weeks or months, from sowing to harvesting, seems to make the resulting produce even tastier.

Yet, while many vegetables are foolproof to grow from seed, requiring little more than a drop of water to get them going after they have been popped into a hole in the ground,

Raising aubergines from seed

1 Planting your seeds
Fill a 7.5cm pot with cuttings compost, level and sow a few seeds on the surface.

2 Settling down
Cover seeds with a thin layer of vermiculite or compost. Water and cover with a clear plastic bag.

others require a bit more cosseting before they are ready to go into the garden.

The seeds of some plants need sowing into small pots, which have to be placed in a heated propagator before they will germinate. After they have emerged and have started to grow, the mass of seedlings will need to be split apart and each one transferred carefully to its own pot – a technique old hands call 'pricking out'. After this, the young plant will grow vigorously and may need potting into a series of slightly larger pots before it is ready to brave it outside.

3 Room to move
Once the seeds germinate, remove the rootball from the pot and separate the seedlings without handling the stems.

4 Branching out
Plant each seedling into its own 7.5cm pot, ensuring that the leaves are just above the surface of the compost.

Apart from watering and possibly feeding, depending on what you are growing, some types of vegetable may also need staking or even pruning to ensure you end up with a well-branched plant.

Growing from seed is not as complicated as it sounds; as your skills as a gardener develop, growing from seed will become as easy as riding a bike – after a few wobbly moments you'll quickly build up confidence and find yourself sowing with gusto. When you reach this point, you can join the legions of seasoned gardeners who get a big kick out of browsing through the seed catalogues, issued by mail-order nurseries, or scanning the displays in garden centres and picking from the hundreds of varieties available.

But what should you do if your green fingers are still developing? If you can't devote the necessary time to nurture seedlings? Or if you simply don't have the space to grow from seed? Well, don't despair; there are several 'cheats' to guarantee you will still have plenty of tasty crops to tuck into, but that require less time, effort and space.

Although there's less choice of variety than growing from seed, many vegetables are available as plug plants from mail-order nurseries or from your local garden centre. Growers fill special trays or modules, which contain a

Pot up mail order plants as soon as they arrive.

number of 'cells', with compost and then sow a seed into each one. Young plants are then sold to gardeners after they have germinated and the roots have filled the cell. Some plugs are tiny, but others are quite chunky and are often sold as 'jumbo' plugs.

A well-grown plug plant tomato.

Vegetables such as tomatoes, cucumbers, onions, broad beans, spinach, garlic, lettuce, leeks, French beans, cabbages and beetroot are available in this way. Although this list is not exhaustive and you can track down lots more vegetable types by checking the stocklists and catalogues of specialist vegetable growers.

While plug plants do save you the bother or sowing and pricking out, if you buy them too early in the season some tender vegetables, like tomatoes and peppers for example, will still require potting on several times and will also need to be kept under cover until they are ready to be planted out once the frosts are over for the year. To avoid this, buy larger plants in pots in late spring, which you can put outside straight away.

A recent introduction are grafted vegetable plants, where two varieties of a vegetable are united to make a single plant. For instance, the bottom (rootstock) of a vigorous variety of tomato can be attached, by machine, to the top of a variety of tomato known for its tasty fruit. The result is a fast-growing, productive plant that produces a great-tasting crop. As these plants grow strongly, they are also more able to withstand disease than other vegetables. At present there is only a fairly limited range of grafted vegetables for sale – tomatoes, peppers, aubergines, cucumbers and melons – but plenty more are likely to be available in the future as they are developed.

Do bear in mind, when choosing to buy young plants, that, due to the technology and work involved in growing them, young plants in pots are much more expensive than those sold in garden centres that have been grown from seed, or indeed than sowing seed yourself.

How to sow seeds

Vegetable seeds need sowing at different depths and spacing depending on the variety, but the process of sowing is more or less the same whatever you decide to grow. Seeds are either sown in shallow, straight trenches, known as drills, or simply scattered across the surface in a process known as broadcast sowing.

Generally, vegetables are sown in drills. Growing this way makes the best use of the available space and allows you access to harvest and maintain the plants easily. Before sowing, tie a length of twine to two garden canes at either end of the plot – when this is stretched taut it will act as a

Seeds need sowing in drills or shallow trenches.

guide to ensure you sow seeds in a straight line, rather than in a trench that meanders all over the place.

To make your first drill, place the canes in the ground at a set distance apart with the string a fraction above the surface of the soil. Rows can either be long or short, depending on your space and the design of your vegetable garden. Slip the first tine of a rake under the string and angle its head so a corner is touching the soil, then draw the rake towards you making a trench (the depth depends on what you are sowing, so check the guide here or look on the back of the seed packet).

If conditions are wet it helps to add a layer of sand to the bottom of the trench before sowing, so the seeds aren't sitting in water that could cause them to rot. In very dry conditions, trickle water along the base of the trench first. After sowing at the correct depth and spacing, draw the soil that was excavated from the trench back over the seeds and tap gently with the head of the rake to make certain the seeds are in contact with the soil. An alternative to making a drill, when sowing large seeds, is to use a dibber to make holes at the correct spacing and depth along your line.

Broadcast sowing is used less frequently and is not suitable for most crops, but the method can be used to sow a designated area with mixed salad leaves, radishes and carrots. Simply sow by scattering the seeds thinly over the soil, rake into the surface gently and water with a watering can fitted with a rose to ensure a fine spray. After they have germinated, the seedlings will need thinning out to allow each one space to grow.

Planting out

Seedlings, plugs and fully grown plants should be planted into a well-prepared seed bed. Most can be planted outside in spring, after the danger of frost has passed and when they have up to six true leaves. If you buy plug plants of tender specimens early in the season, these will need to be potted up and protected under glass until they can be safely

Ensure plants are correctly spaced out to allow them to grow.

After planting ensure plants romp away by watering well.

taken outside. If your plug plants arrive at the correct time for planting, plant them out immediately or they will suffer.

To plant, water plants well and then dig a hole in the soil with a trowel. Decant the plant from the pot and, holding it gently by its leaves, lower it into the hole. The surface of the compost rootball should be just beneath the level of the soil. Draw the soil back into the hole around the rootball and firm it in gently with your fingertips. After planting, soak the soil well.

Crop rotation

Mention crop rotation and it sounds like some complicated technique carried out by those with years of vegetable-growing experience, but at its most basic it simply means growing different sorts of annual crops in a different spot every year.

There are a variety of reasons why vegetable gardeners aim to do this; the most important being that it reduces the risk of specific pests and diseases building up in the same spot, and it allows plants to mop up the nutrients left in the soil by others.

Although there are a number of ways to rotate crops, the simplest method is to divide your growing area into three and then split the plants into three groups to be moved methodically on an annual cycle to a bed they have not grown in previously.

Divide your crops into beans and fruit (runner beans, broad beans, tomatoes, peppers, sweetcorn, lettuces, aubergines and peas), brassicas (broccoli, cabbages, kale and radishes) and root veg (potatoes, onions, beetroots, carrots and sweet potatoes). Grow each in a designated area, then the following year grow brassicas where the beans and fruit were, root veg where the brassicas were, and beans and fruit in the gap left by the root veg. The next year rotate again, and then in year four the crops will be back where they started.

While a crop-rotation scheme makes good growing sense in allotments and larger vegetable patches, lack of space means it is much harder to put it into practice in smaller gardens, and so may not be a viable technique.

Dividing a garden into beds makes crop rotation easy.

Keep them moving for healthy plants

Moving brassicas around is extremely important as they can suffer from clubroot, a fungal disease that resides in the soil and causes stunted growth and plants to die. By ensuring they grow in a different spot each year, you can prevent the disease building up underground. Beans also absorb nitrogen from the air and trap the nutrient in their roots, so after the crop dies, nitrogen resides in the soil and can be taken up by the next crop. Therefore, it's good to follow them with hungry plants, such as brassicas.

Planning to bridge the 'hungry gap'

It's incredibly easy to have a vegetable patch that provides you with handfuls of fresh produce from summer to late autumn, as the bulk of annual vegetables are ready for sowing or planting in the spring. Even after autumn you can still nosh on vegetables you have managed to store well into winter. However, it's harder to ensure that a patch of soil earns its keep in the other half of the year, but not impossible, and it's a good idea to keep a plot of land as productive as possible so you have crops to pick and eat all year round.

If you have space, include a few perennial crops that will remain in the same spot all year round. After harvesting your spring-sown crops in late summer or early autumn, aim to sow seeds or plants to fill the 'hungry gap' – a six-week period from about mid-April – when there's generally nothing to unearth, pick or cut.

Most crops aren't suitable for growing through the winter months, so you won't suffer from headaches as you prepare a decidedly short planting list. Crops that can be raised successfully include spinach, chard, leeks, spring cabbages, broad beans, purple sprouting broccoli and kale.

There aren't many podded vegetables that can be grown over winter, but several varieties of broad bean are ideal. Those that are best for sowing in mid to late autumn, for an early spring crop, include 'Aquadulce', 'Super Aquadulce' and 'Claudia Aquadulce'. Although you would traditionally sow peas in the spring, it is possible to produce an early crop by sowing 'Kelvedon Wonder' on light land after Christmas and protecting the emerging seedlings with a tunnel cloche.

Right **Sow broad beans in autumn for an early spring crop.**
Far right **Leeks are a welcome crop in winter.**

Many brassicas will provide pickings during late spring. Try the aptly named kale 'Hungry Gap' or sow spring cabbages in August for an early crop. If you want to try something different, go for 'Hispi' – a pointed cabbage that can be sown in January or February and will produce hearting cabbages with a delicious flavour from summer until autumn.

For a steady supply of leafy crops from winter into spring, sow brightly coloured chard in late summer, or lettuces like 'Winter Density' or 'Rouge d'Hiver'. For more unusual salads, sow oriental plants, such as pak choi, tatsoi and mustard greens. Another interesting variety is claytonia, or miner's lettuce, which can be sown in August and treated as a cut-and-come-again crop. All of these will need protecting against the worst of the weather with a cloche.

Tools of the trade

Head to your local garden centre or DIY store and you'll be confronted with a bewildering array of different tools; some you will immediately recognize and others look like weapons from a medieval armoury. If you were to snap up everything on offer it would leave a large hole in your pocket, but fortunately you only need a handful of tools to grow your own vegetables.

A spade is essential for digging the soil, especially if you have a lot of it, like an allotment, for example. Choose the

Plan carefully so you have edibles to pick in winter and early spring.

best you can afford, as a good-quality tool will make digging easier and will be an investment because it should last a lifetime. The best blades are made from stainless steel and will have either a D-shaped or T-shaped handle. D-shapes can be uncomfortable when used over a long period of time, while a T-shaped handle is more comfortable and is a better fit for a larger pair of hands. Test your spade in the shop before buying it. They come with different length shanks and you should choose one that feels comfortable for your height, requiring the least amount of stooping when using.

A fork is very useful for fluffing up soil that has been previously dug with a spade, prising plants from the ground, or lifting certain vegetable crops from the soil without damaging them, such as potatoes. The same buying criteria for spades applies to forks.

Seeds need sowing into a level bed of soil that resembles breadcrumbs. To end up with this texture you will need a steel-headed garden rake with solid teeth, which is either mounted on a wooden or metal handle. Rakes come with heads in different sizes. If you only have a small area that needs raking, go for a model with a narrow head of around

Store tools neatly so you can find them easily.

24cm (9in), while large patches can be quickly cultivated using a rake with a head of around 30cm (12in). Apart from preparing seed beds, rakes are also useful for levelling soil or removing any debris that falls onto the soil in the vegetable garden.

Hoes are useful tools for controlling weeds without resorting to chemical controls. There are several different types available, but the most common are Dutch, or push, hoes and draw, or pull, hoes. Dutch hoes are generally pushed backwards and forwards and are ideal for slicing through the top of weeds and for precise weeding around plants. A draw hoe is pulled towards you, dragging the weed from the ground – the corner of a draw hoe is also useful for making shallow trenches when sowing seeds. Both are useful in their own way, and over time you might want to include one of each in your tool shed. But if you're starting out, go for a Dutch hoe, as it is by far the most useful.

Apart from these larger tools, the other essentials that you will use on a regular basis are a watering can, a ball of garden twine, a wheelbarrow (a trug or bucket will do if you only have a small garden), a hand trowel for digging planting holes and a pair of secateurs, which can be used for pruning and cutting twine. A pair of bypass secateurs is best, as they will have blades that last longer than those of the anvil types.

Seed-sowing tools

Sowing seeds is made easier when you have the right tools. A heated propagator is essential for germinating seeds early in the season. These come in all different shapes and sizes, with some being relatively cheap to buy and top-end models having a price tag that would make you wince. Firstly, buy a model that will fit in your allotted area. They need a light spot, such as a greenhouse or a windowsill, so make sure you have room for it. If you only plan to grow a few plants from seed, there's little point in shelling out on an expensive propagator when a cheap one will do just as well.

When pricking out seedlings a small wooden tool, known sometimes as a dibblet, is handy. Roughly around the size of a pencil, it has a pointed end for making holes in compost and can be used to help lift a seedling when transplanting and dropping it carefully into the hole. A wooden dibber (basically a larger dibblet that tapers from top to bottom)

Buying second-hand tools

Although top-quality, brand new tools are desirable, they are not essential. If price is an issue, or you need to leave tools at the allotment and need a second set as you are concerned they might get stolen, you can easily find tools that cost a fraction of the price of those in the shops. Second-hand shops, junk stores and car-boot sales are a great source of used tools that might have seen better days, but still have plenty of life left in them.

is equally valuable when you need to make larger holes in either the ground or pots of compost when you are planting plugs or larger seedlings.

Tool care

It may sound like obvious advice, but tools will last longer if you look after them. Why spend your hard-earned cash on kitting out your tool shed if you are going to leave everything lying around to get rusty or for wooden parts to weather and rot? You don't need to do anything elaborate, simply knock off any lumps of soil and give them a wipe over with a dry cloth if they are wet. Secateurs work better if they are sharp, obviously, so occasionally sharpen the blade with a wet stone.

Where to grow

Whether you've got a few acres out in the countryside or just a balcony attached to a high-rise city flat you can still grow vegetables. Those with oodles of space or an allotment can really go to town and grow a wide variety of crops, while those who can step out their back door and almost reach the bottom of the garden with an outstretched hand will have to be more modest about the choice of veg that they grow.

Smaller spaces

Not everyone has an allotment or large garden in which they can hive off a corner to raise copious amounts of vegetables. But lack of space doesn't mean you can't grow your own – far from it. Pots, hanging baskets, growing bags and other types of container can be squeezed into the tightest of spaces, while climbing vegetables can be grown against walls or even up the protective railings that surround a balcony. Obviously, you could never expect to be self-sufficient when you are so strapped for space, but you can still grow enough to perk up several meals.

Growing in pots

Many edibles will thrive in containers. Often they don't take up much space, which makes them perfect for patios, balconies and roof gardens.

The key to successfully growing plants in pots is to choose containers that are large enough for your plants (20–45cm (8–18in) in diameter is ideal) and have drainage holes in the base. There are lots to choose from; plastic pots are cheap, while frost-proof terracotta looks great, but dries out quickly (this can be remedied by lining them with plastic

With careful planning, you can use the smallest container to support several plants.

sheeting that is pierced at the base). You can also recycle old food containers, wooden crates or galvanized metal buckets to grow vegetables in.

When filling pots, either use a soil-based John Innes No. 2 compost or a multi-purpose compost, and arrange pots together in a sunny spot.

Growing in hanging baskets and window boxes

If you live in a flat or don't have a garden, don't despair. You can still grow vegetables in hanging baskets and window boxes, which will also make the most of any vertical space.

The best vegetables for hanging baskets are those that have a naturally cascading habit, or that remain fairly compact. Tumbling varieties of tomato are perfect and so easy to pick when they are raised off the ground. Alternatively, try dwarf French beans or sow salad leaves. Whatever basket you choose, and there are lots of different styles and materials on the market, ensure that the basket bracket is secured firmly to the wall to avoid a nasty accident involving falling pots.

Window boxes generally have a bit more room inside them than baskets, so you can squeeze in more vegetables. Spring onions, salad leaves and radishes are the perfect candidates for growing this way and can be sown in short rows across the width of the box. You can also add baby or stump-rooted carrots, beetroots and tumbling tomatoes. Avoid anything that gets too tall though, as they will look out of scale and could become top heavy, resulting in the box moving during windy weather. Just like with hanging baskets, keep safety in mind. Secure the box to prevent it moving and avoid water running out of the drainage hole by placing a saucer or tray beneath the box.

Far left **Grow your own peppers in pots.**
Left **Trailing varieties of tomatoes are perfect for hanging baskets.**

Growing bags

Compact growing bags are ideal in situations where you don't have a lot of space. They can be pushed up against a wall on a sunny patio, against a fence or placed on a balcony or terrace. Despite measuring just 35 x 95cm (14 x 37in), each has enough space for three vegetable plants and they are ideal for crops that don't have deep roots, such as peppers, cucumbers, aubergines, courgettes and tomatoes. By cutting a long panel in the top it's also possible to use a bag for raising salads.

Preparing a growing bag

Why is it necessary to explain how to prepare a growing bag? Surely all you have to do is just make some holes in the top and add your plants? Almost, but you do have to do a little bit more to ensure that your plants thrive, rather than just limp along sadly. When you buy a new bag you'll find they are usually flat and the compost inside is compacted. Planting directly into this is almost certainly bound to end in disaster, so fluff up the compost by kneading the bag, making sure you break up any clumps. Shape the bag into a low hummock, then slash the sides of the bag near the bottom a few times to allow excess moisture to drain away.

Prepare growing bags correctly before planting.

The top of the bag will have some pre-marked planting squares. Cut these out carefully and remove some compost from each, leaving holes large enough for the root balls of your plants. Place a plant in each hole and then return the extracted compost, firming it in and around each one.

When you've finished, each rootball should be covered with compost and be sitting beneath the surface of the bag.

If you are planning to grow salads in a growing bag, prepare as before, but ignore the pre-marked planting squares. Cut out a rectangular panel along the top of the bag and sow in short rows across the width.

Try to recycle your growing bag. After harvesting summer tomatoes, lift the plants and sift through the compost to remove as many roots as you can. Add a little fresh compost, then use the bag for raising salads in the autumn. Don't be tempted to re-use the bag the following year, as all the nutrients will have been exhausted by then.

Raised beds

A raised bed is a bit like a giant container, but it has several advantages over growing in pots. You can raise more crops than you can easily grow in pots, and having a specific site for vegetables makes managing your crops easier. It makes a great design feature and by not growing everything in pots, which are generally dotted about all over the place, you free up much-needed space in the garden.

Make raised beds deep enough for your chosen crops.

Making a raised bed

1 Marking the joints
Beds can be any size, but 90cm wide is ideal. Cut four pieces of timber, and mark slots 10cm from the side on all pieces.

2 Jigsaw cutting
Secure the timber with a clamp and carefully cut out the slots. The slots should be just wider than the timber.

Essentially a square or rectangular frame filled with a compost mix, a raised bed can be made from a pile of old bricks, untreated railway sleepers or from newly bought timber. Alternatively, you can buy kits, which are really simple to slot together. Although they can be made up to waist height, a 90cm (35in) square bed with 23cm (9in) high sides is ideal for most gardens.

Place your bed in a sunny, sheltered spot, and if you like you can also stick a band of copper tape around the outside to deter greedy slugs and snails – they will get a sharp

3 **Slotting together**
Slot all four lengths of timber together to make a square frame.

4 **Adding the finishing touch**
After it has been constructed, fill your raised bed with a mixture of compost and top soil.

electric shock as they pass over the tape, which will help safeguard your plants from attack.

Square-foot garden

Square-foot gardening is a technique that makes the most of a raised bed. Rather than simply growing vegetables ad hoc, you can split up a bed into 30cm (12in) squares and grow a different vegetable in each. You can make the beds any size you wish, but if you have a really tiny garden, try a 90 x 90cm (3 x 3ft) raised bed, and divide it into a grid of

nine squares. To do this you can either mark the surface of the compost with a cane, or hammer nails along the outside of the frame and run strings across to form a grid pattern.

Put the bed in a light, sunny place on a lawn, deck or patio and fill it with your compost mix – 50 per cent top soil with 50 per cent multi-purpose compost, along with a few handfuls of horticultural grit to improve drainage is the perfect balance.

When planting, be careful to choose varieties that are low growing, compact, and that do not spread too much. Peppers, beetroots, salad leaves, Swiss chard, dwarf French beans, aubergines, spring onions and radishes are perfect. Salads should be sown in short rows in the squares, while a single vegetable plant, grown for its fruit should be planted in the centre of a square. For leafy crops, such as basil, space out four plants in a square.

After planting, water well and cover the bed with a sheet of chicken wire to deter cats, who may think it is an open-air litter tray. The wire can be removed when the plants are actively growing.

A different vegetable is grown in each square.

Making the most of a greenhouse

Growing crops outdoors is fine in summer, but as the days shorten, temperatures drop and light levels fall you'll find that all but the hardiest crops struggle or even get turned to mush by the merest mention of the word frost. If you have a small greenhouse, make the most of it by growing crops in this protected environment from early autumn. Growing bags or pots can be planted with mixed salad leaves, mizuna, rocket, winter purslane, corn salad, radishes or lettuce. Give the plants the lightest spot possible, raising them up on greenhouse benches or staging if necessary. Keep plants moist, but not soaking wet, to avoid the spread of fungal diseases.

When you've got more room

When you're not hamstrung by space you can grow many more vegetables. By choosing varieties carefully and planning for growing all year round you could become self-sufficient or, if you are not producing all your own vegetables, you should be aiming to grow enough to add to every meal for at least part of the year.

Kit your greenhouse out with benches, shelves and staging to make the most of your space.

However, despite being able to enjoy growing and eating many more different varieties, there is a downside. Growing crops on a larger scale means you have more responsibility than gardeners with vegetable patches the size of a postage stamp. All the plants will need looking after and the more you have, the more time it will take to maintain them and the plot. Wherever and whenever you can, take steps to save yourself time, whether it's mulching between plants to suppress weeds or choosing varieties that need the minimum amount of upkeep.

Kitchen gardens

Historically, self-contained kitchen gardens were created to provide stately homes with vegetables, fruit and flowers, and were often found hidden behind four mighty brick walls. Today, a self-contained kitchen garden is likely to be a far more humble affair. It might still be walled, but many kitchen gardens that are built from scratch will be surrounded by far cheaper partition alternatives, such as hedges, or even a fruiting barrier, such as step-over apples. In towns or cities, where there is less space, a kitchen

A well-planned kitchen garden should keep you in produce for much of the year.

garden could be enclosed by trellis screens, which could be used to support climbing vegetables.

Although you could plant vegetables in rows, it's a much better idea to divide the ground into rectangular sections separated by paths or even with a series of rectangular raised beds. Doing this makes maintaining plants easier and the divisions mean that diseases and pests can't spread as rapidly as they would if the plants were in long lines.

If you are creating a kitchen garden from scratch, plan it carefully on squared paper. Mark the outline and then the position of paths and beds, ensuring you have enough of them to be able to operate a crop rotation system. The paths need to be wide enough for a wheelbarrow, and could be made from grass or built with bricks or gravel.

When planning your site, make sure you include somewhere for storing tools and materials, an area for composting and somewhere you can install a water point.

Allotment

If you have the time to maintain it, an allotment is the perfect place for people with small gardens who want to grow lots of crops. However, a mistake made by many first-time allotment holders is to do too much in their first

A shed is essential on an allotment to keep your tools and gardening kit.

season. Unless you can visit your plot on a daily basis to
water, weed and maintain plants, you are best using just
a fraction of your plot with the aim of expanding slowly
each year.

Rather than plant up the whole plot, make life easy for
yourself by using a third of the available space and cover the
rest with sheets of black landscape fabric, or even pieces of
old carpet, until you are ready to use the soil.

Traditionally, on allotments vegetables are grown in rows, but again, raised beds are ideal if you want to grow crops on boggy ground or have a plot with clay soil. Gardening this way also helps save you time and labour – paths in between the beds can be covered with strips of landscape fabric and then spread with either bark chippings or gravel, thereby reducing the area that requires weeding and attention from you.

Beds measuring 2.5 x 1.2m (8 x 4ft) are ideal, allowing you to easily reach into the centre for harvesting. All you need to make a raised bed is four lengths of timber for the sides and four short lengths of 5 x 5cm (2 x 2in) timber to use as corner posts. Don't worry about using a spirit level and tape measure to get perfect shapes, allotment growing is rough and ready and doesn't need precision, so simply nail the pieces together to make a rectangle.

Aim for a minimum depth of 15cm (6in), but if you want to grow root crops, such as carrots and parsnips, the sides of the bed will need to be around 30cm (12in) high, while potatoes need beds about 38cm (15in) deep. There are no set rules about what you should fill the bed with, but a mixture of top soil and garden compost works well.

Growing in beds and borders

You don't need to redesign your entire garden in order to be able to enjoy fresh vegetables. Beds and borders often have gaps in them, which can be plugged by adding edible plants. Many vegetables have attractive leaves, flowers and fruit, or they have architectural good looks so they don't look out of place when grown among perennials or shrubs in the garden. Sweetcorn are good fillers for the middle or back of the border and can be used like annual grasses, while purple- or yellow-podded beans make an eye-catching statement when grown up an ornamental obelisk. Leafy crops like kale 'Black Tuscany', kale 'Redbor' and ruby chard are superb for adding a very attractive dash of colour to a plot.

Salads are great for plugging a tight gap, even in semi-shade, and they will also prevent weeds from colonizing these patches of bare soil. Mixed salad leaves can be grown in short rows or even broadcast sown in these areas. Alternatively, plant a single lettuce and let it grow until it fills the space.

Before planting anything, make sure you 'tickle' the soil with a fork and rake it over well to leave a fine finish.

Potager

While different vegetables can be grown cheek by jowl, you can make a more decorative display by mixing them with perennial and annual flowers in a potager – a style of garden that originates from the kitchen gardens of France.

Rather than planting in serried rows, the aim with a potager is to mix attractive-looking fruit, vegetables and herbs with ornamental plants in a series of square or rectangular beds. In these gardens, plants are chosen carefully to complement each other, often through a co-ordinated colour scheme.

Sometimes these beds are delineated by clipped box or lavender plants, or by lengths of chunky hardwood or even sleepers. Although structurally formal, after planting the geometric outlines are lost as plants are allowed to knit together and spill over the edges.

As with other styles of gardening, you should aim to make the most of the vertical space too. Add obelisks or wigwams for growing beans and gourds, making sure these and any other tall plants are near the centre of the bed with the height of plants graduating down towards the outside.

Mix vegetables, fruit and flowers together for an ornamental, but productive garden.

Choosing the right varieties

For the first time veg grower, choosing what to grow can be like playing 'pin the tail on the donkey'. Flick through the pages of any seed catalogue and you'll be confronted with an A–Z (zucchini, if you were wondering – the Italian word for courgette) of different vegetables, with many varieties of each. An average seed catalogue may contain around 40 varieties of tomato, for example, so how do you make a decision about what to grow when you might only have space for one or two plants?

Well, there's no real mystery to this. You do whatever every other gardener does: read the descriptions and make a choice based on its looks, taste and whether it's suited to the space you can offer it – whether that's a hanging basket, window box, growing bag against a wall or a patch of bare earth at an allotment.

If space is not an issue you can grow a wide range of crops.

Vegetables suited to your garden

Apart from being guided by a description you might read in a catalogue or on the back of a seed packet, you need to bear other things in mind. The vegetables should be ones you like to eat and the varieties of those vegetables should be suited to your space, whether you've got a window box or a few rolling acres complete with a walled kitchen garden. If you've been put off growing crops in the past because of pests and diseases, you could consider varieties that will shrug off any problems without complaint, allowing you to enjoy a harvest without spending months tackling a fungal problem that might threaten to wipe out your crop.

Deciding what to grow is fun – pick the right varieties for you and your space and your first venture into growing your own will be a resounding success.

To suggest growing crops that suit the amount of space you have may sound like obvious advice, but you'd be surprised how often this recommendation is ignored.

For example, sweetcorn is a plant that grows very tall and is best suited to growing in an allotment or large vegetable patch, where you can plant a big block of them. They are pollinated by the wind, so they need other plants around them to ensure this is carried out successfully. As each plant only carries between one and two cobs, you will only get a worthwhile crop if you grow enough of them. Still, this doesn't stop some space-strapped gardeners giving them a go, and planting a single towering plant in a pot. However, if you want a maximum harvest from a minimal space, you're better off planting up pots with plants that crop quickly, rather than with one plant that requires the entire pot from spring to early autumn with the only reward at the end of this time being one cob – if you're lucky.

So, if you're planning on growing your own in pots, choose vegetables that are suited to such a confined space. Generally, these will be plants that are dwarf, compact, don't become too top heavy, or need a great depth of compost in order to develop. Plants that don't have any of these attributes tend to sulk in pots; they need constant watering, frequent re-potting, regular feeding and tend to get bashed about by the wind and need picking up after the slightest gust. The end result is an unhealthy plant whose crop is far poorer than it would have been if it had been growing happily in the ground.

Right **Salads thrive in pots.**
Far right **Stump-rooted carrots are perfect for containers.**

Gardeners with bags of space can pick from a wider range of plants, of course. If you want, you can grow all these compact crops too, but you also have the luxury of being able to try your hand at growing plants that would never survive in pots. Choose from a diverse range of crops, such as cauliflowers, Brussels sprouts, leeks, sweetcorn, Jerusalem artichokes, asparagus, globe artichokes, marrows, pumpkins and squashes.

Grow what you like to eat

Growing veg is great fun, and after you've had success growing a few from seed there can be a tendency to increase your output by growing all manner of crops. While many of these might be things you like to eat, the chances are that some will be plants you decide to grow just to try out your new gardening skills. Trying new things is one of the joys of growing your own – it gives you the opportunity to grow tomatillos, mooli and other vegetables that you are unlikely to see in your average food store. However, avoid plants that you and your family don't like to eat. There's no point in dedicating time and space to a plant that will end up on the compost heap.

Choosing crops for taste

Apart from picking crops that suit the space available, a key rule for many is to choose crops that you enjoy and that taste good. Although you could argue, quite rightly, that anything you have lovingly grown will taste better than a crop that was picked, flung into a cold store and shipped halfway across the country (or sometimes the world) before hitting the supermarket shelf, you should still try to pick vegetables that will get even the most long-in-the-tooth chef salivating.

Often, but not always, gourmet vegetables are heritage varieties that aren't widely known about or that have been superseded by modern varieties that are considered to be more vigorous, easier to grow or have a greater resistance to specific pests and diseases. Although you obviously want to raise your vegetables with the least amount of trouble, don't rule out these heritage plants as they invigorate a meal like nothing else.

Whenever you talk about heritage vegetables you tend to think of tomatoes and potatoes, but in recent years little

Far left **Lettuce is quick, delicious and very easy.**
Left **Home-grown rocket is far tastier than shop-bought leaves.**

known or unusual varieties of both have started to be more widely grown as more nurseries offer them. Bite into a 'Brandywine', 'Ananas Noir' or 'Black Krim' tomato and you'll enjoy a combination of complex flavours that are unlike anything you've tasted before. These, and the other tomatoes you'll find within the pages of a decent seed catalogue, have a smoky taste; others are sweet, and some are incredibly rich or have a slightly citrus taste. Apart from the fact that they are naturally far tastier than the dull varieties that are grown en masse for supermarkets, those nurtured in your own garden will also benefit from ripening naturally outdoors over a long growing season rather than the commercial crops that have been grown under glass, placed in a cold store and ripened artificially with gasses.

Potatoes can be equally full of flavour and a delight to serve up. Seed catalogues offer dozens of varieties that are far more tempting than the usual red or white option you might be confronted with in a shop. Why should your taste buds put up with such mediocre spuds, when they could be dancing to the nutty flavour of a knobby 'Anya' or a tasty 'Edzell Blue'?

Potatoes are ideal in both small and large gardens.

If you enjoy eating beans you should try growing borlotti beans – a delicacy that is highly prized by Italians who, let's face it, know a thing or two about food. The red-and-white flecked pods are eaten whole when immature, or the speckled beans can be shelled and dried when mature. Climbing varieties like 'Lamon', which is the bean most commonly used in the famous dish *pasta e fagioli*, are best grown in a raised bed, vegetable patch or allotment – either up a wigwam of canes or in rows 15cm (6in) apart, with 50cm (20in) between the rows and using canes as supports. 'Saluggia' and other dwarf varieties can be planted 10cm (4in) apart in large pots with a few twiggy sticks to prevent them from collapsing. The beans can be picked from late summer, when the pods start to crack.

Another gourmet crop worth seeking out is beetroot 'Chioggia'. This looks and tastes unlike any other beetroot and is a firm favourite among celebrity chefs. From the outside it looks like any other purple-skinned beetroot, but cut it open and you'll find concentric rings of red and white, which fade to a pink colour when cooked. The flesh is very succulent and sweet.

Borlotti beans are a true delicacy.

Some perennials are worth including, if you have the space. Artichokes are a delicacy, but are costly to buy in supermarkets. A single plant will provide you with more than enough globe-shaped heads, but the plant can grow to 2m (6ft) and have a substantial spread. If you have an allotment with a vacant sunny spot you could consider planting one. Once it gets going it requires very little upkeep, other than regular watering.

Aubergines have become popular vegetables in recent years. There are some wonderful varieties that are worth tracking down, which are a cut above the rest of the purple tribe. 'Listada de Gandia' produce large, pale purple fruit that are attractively streaked with white and have an excellent flavour, while 'Violetta Lunga' has extra-long fruit that are perfect for the Italian aubergine and parmesan dish of *melanzane alla parmigiana*.

Really fast crops for those in a hurry

Not everyone has the patience to nurture a crop that requires oodles of cosseting for several months before it is ready to harvest. Many folk lead busy lives with work

Salad leaves can be picked within weeks of sowing.

or family, or both, and have other interests that keep them
occupied leaving very little time for the garden. So, if this is
true of you, should you give up all aspiration to grow your
own? Absolutely not, you just simply need to grow plants
that require the minimum of care and grow really quickly, so
that you have the opportunity to grow something else when
they've been harvested, or to take a rain check for a few
weeks before starting again.

Peppery radish is a fast favourite.

Mixed salad leaves are the ultimate fast crop – the vegetable equivalent of a Formula-1 racing champion. There are so many different varieties to choose from, ranging from some that contain a blend of spicy leaves to others that are milder. Apart from the choice, the best thing about these leaves is that three weeks after sowing them in pots, beds or allotments you can start picking them. Other crops that are just as fast are the appropriately named rocket, spicy-leaved mustard and mizuna.

If you don't mind waiting a bit longer there are many other vegetables you could grow. Radishes, spring onions, some varieties of spinach and beetroot are traditional, fast-paced crops, but if you fancy something a bit different, try sowing seeds of baby vegetables. As perfect miniature versions of larger veg, their size means they are ready to pick a lot sooner, often within 6–12 weeks. There are baby kohl rabi, carrots, calabrese, leeks, turnips and even a dwarf French bean, 'Speedy', which has pods that can be picked just seven weeks after sowing.

Alternatively, cheat and buy larger plants that are already developing, such as tomatoes, peppers and aubergines. You'll miss out on the nurturing stage, but you will still be able to enjoy watching lots of fresh produce ripen for harvesting.

Disease-free vegetables

If you grow your own vegetables you will need to deal with pests and diseases at some stage. It's inevitable, unfortunately. But if you want to reduce the time you spend trying to sort out problems, you could consider growing crops that are naturally resistant or that have been bred to be more tolerant of certain pests and diseases.

Potatoes can succumb to blight, a fungal disease that can wipe out crops if it gets a hold, usually in warm and wet summers. Although it's possible to spray crops as a precaution, there has been much work carried out by breeders in recent years to introduce varieties that are more resistant to blight. Although not entirely immune, varieties such as 'Sarpo Mira', 'Sarpa Axona' and 'Red Cara' grow so vigorously that they are much better able to cope with blight so the disease is unlikely to be entirely detrimental to the harvest.

Tomatoes can also fall foul of blight, which can damage both foliage and fruit, but new varieties with better vigour are showing great tolerance to this disease. 'Legend' and

Right and far right **Blight is a problem with tomatoes, but can be avoided by growing a disease resistant variety, such as Ferline.**

'Lupitas' all have excellence tolerance, as does 'Ferline', which also has good natural resistance to fusarium and verticilium wilt.

Carrot fly is a major pest for carrots, laying eggs that turn into maggots, which make the root inedible. You can protect against it by covering the crop with mesh to stop the fly reaching the crop, and the risk can be even more reduced by sowing seeds of resistant carrots. Good varieties include 'Flyaway' and 'Resistafly' – both of these have lower levels

of chlorogenic acid, a substance within the developing root that attracts the attention of the fly. As a further precaution against the pest you could grow a carrot variety alongside the resistant types that does attract them; by sacrificing this crop the roots of the resistant varieties stay clean. Alternatively, plant a few onions among the carrots, as their strong scent deters the fly.

Courgettes are one of the most productive vegetables you can grow, but they are vulnerable to several diseases. Cucumber mosaic virus can cause crop failure, although 'Defender' is resistant to this. 'Dario', 'Firenze', 'Tuscany' and 'Segev' are all resistant to another disease: powdery mildew.

Other vegetables that shrug off problems include the cabbage 'Kilaton', which is club-root resistant, and the spinaches 'Toscane' and 'Fiorano', which are both resistant to mildew.

Downy mildew is a fungal disease that can be recognized by brownish patches on the upper side of leaves and white mould on the underside. The disease prospers in the damp, humid conditions that occur when plants are grown too close together. Sow or grow at the correct spacing and don't overwater to avoid problems. If plants get downy mildew, pick off the infected leaves or spray it with fungicide. Plants that show tolerance to downy mildew are peas 'Avola', 'Kelvedon Wonder' and 'Greenshaft', which is also tolerant to fusarium wilt. If you find your lettuces have succumbed to downy mildew, try 'Pandero', 'Chartwell' or 'Cassandra'. These varieties are also resistant to lettuce mosaic virus, which is spread by aphids and results in mottled and puckered leaves. The only way to tackle it is to remove infected plants and control the aphids to prevent its spread.

Fusarium wilt is a fungal disease that can cause soft stems to droop, eventually leading to entire plants dying. There is no chemical cure, so you must remove the entire plant and not grow any closely related plants in the same bed for five years, as the spores of the fungus can remain in the soil all that time.

Choose crops to suit your experience

While it is easy to recommend crops you really should grow, it's also necessary to suggest plants that you shouldn't grow as a beginner. Many fantastic vegetables need lots of care and attention, so they are best left to attempt when your

Top of the crops

Often you'll see the letters F1 printed after the name of the vegetables on a seed packet. F1 indicates that the plant has been created as the result of crossing two inbred, sterile parent lines. The important thing for the gardener to know is that F1 seeds produce uniform plants that are vigorous and high yielding; so these are good seeds for beginners. However, you can't save the seed after flowering to use in subsequent years as the resulting plants won't breed true from their own seeds.

fingers have really turned green. For instance, home-grown cucumbers are a real treat, with a taste far superior than anything from the supermarket. There are so many varieties to pick from that reading the seed catalogues can make you impatient to get growing. But here's the downside: this crop is vulnerable to vagaries of temperature, watering and can be extremely temperamental. It also needs to have lots of attention paid to feeding, supporting and pruning, and some even need their flowers removed on a regular basis. Therefore this is not a crop to start off with, but rather something to look forward to growing in the future.

Cucumbers taste great, but are very tricky to grow.

Some crops, such as parsnips, are so cheap to buy from a market that you should question whether it is worth spending a large amount of time and effort planting and nurturing them. Others spend most of the year in situ as they mature, taking up a lot of space that could be put aside for faster-cropping varieties. Among those that fall into this category, and that you might want to avoid (unless you have a real penchant for them), are cauliflowers, cabbages, Brussels sprouts and leeks.

Whatever you decide to grow, choose the varieties carefully. For instance, why go for a bog-standard potato that you could find in any shop or market, when you could grow an unusual heritage variety that will turn an ordinary meal into something really special? And why find space in the garden for varieties of tomato that are similar to those you might pick up on a regular basis from a supermarket when there are hundreds of interesting varieties to grow? From historic tomatoes that were grown by gardeners a century or so ago, to those that are unusually shaped or coloured and can provide a real talking point.

So, if you want to tantalize your taste buds and impress all of those that visit your garden – and possibly your kitchen – grow something exciting.

Far left **Cauliflowers take a long time to reach maturity.**
Left **Sprouts need a lot of space to grow.**

Foolproof veg

There are so many vegetables worth growing that it's difficult to pick just a handful for the first time veg grower to try. To make the choice a little easier, in this directory are 16 vegetables that are popular for eating and that you could grow with your eyes shut – although some do require a bit more TLC than others. After mastering the growing techniques for these plants you'll soon feel up for growing more unusual or challenging crops.

Beetroot

Fresh beetroot is a completely different taste sensation when compared to the limp slices you often see swimming in vinegar. Earthy and deliciously tender, beetroot is a doddle to grow in a sunny spot, and you'll find many tempting varieties to try.

Where to grow

For a worthwhile crop, grow beetroot on an allotment or in a vegetable garden, although you could squeeze a row into a raised bed. Beetroot can also be grown in pots and a large container will provide a family with enough for two or three meals – cylindrical varieties are the best type to grow in containers as their long straight roots need a deep root run. Baby beets are also ideal for containers.

When to start

Sow seeds directly into moist, fertile soil from late April to July. Early sowings can be made in March, but you must be sure to choose varieties that are suitable for growing at this cooler time.

How to sow seeds

To sow outdoors, directly into the soil, prepare the ground well before sowing by digging it over and removing weeds and large stones. Use a rake to roughly level the surface and then rake vigorously to reduce heavy clods until the soil surface resembles fine breadcrumbs. Use the corner of the rake to make a shallow trench, 2cm (¾in) deep. Drop two seeds into the trench every 10cm (4in), then cover with soil and water in well. Subsequent rows should be spaced 20cm (8in) apart. Once the seeds have germinated, remove the weakest of the two when they are about 2cm (¾in) tall. To ensure a summer-long supply, sow new seeds every month.

If growing in pots, choose a container that is at least 20cm (8in) in diameter and fill it with multi-purpose compost. Firm the soil down and sow seeds fairly thinly across the surface. Cover with 2cm (¾in) of compost and water well. When seedlings are about 2cm (¾in) tall, thin them out leaving 12cm (5in) between the plants so the roots can swell freely.

How to grow

After sowing you can more or less put your feet up, with a few provisos. Simply keep plants well watered, especially during dry spells, and remove any weeds that pop up.

Beetroot are generally ready for harvest about 90 days after sowing, depending on the variety. Pull them up by gently holding the leaves with one hand and levering them up using a hand fork with the other. (Ensure the fork is well under the roots to avoid spearing them.)

What can go wrong?

Growth can be stunted or roots can become woody if the soil is allowed to dry out for long periods. Seeds sown before the recommended time can result in plants bolting or running to seed prematurely, so it is important to sow at the correct

time. However, if you can't wait to get going, pick varieties that are suitable for growing when the weather is cooler.

Varieties to try

Arguably the best tasting, and definitely the most amazing when served up on a plate, is 'Barbabietola di Chioggia', which, when sliced, reveals concentric rings of pink and white. 'Burpee's Golden' has golden skin and flesh, and 'Albina Vereduna' has sweet, white flesh. Good purple beetroots include 'Alto', which has long purple roots, and spherical 'Red Ace', whose roots are a burgundy red. If you're looking for an early, bolt-resistant variety then try 'Boltardy'. 'Pablo' is excellent for pots, producing small baby beets.

Broad beans

Many of us remember the broad beans from our childhood that are best described as being tough as old boots. Yet freshly shelled broad beans that are about the size of your

Far left **'Barbabietola di Chioggia' beetroot being harvested.**
Left **Broad beans produce a prolific crop.**

fingernail are a delicious and tender delicacy. You need space for this crop, but your reward will be heaps of delicious beans that will beat anything you've ever tasted before.

Where to grow

This is really a crop for an allotment or a large vegetable patch, as you need quite a few plants for a decent harvest. If you insist on growing some in containers you can get away with a shorter variety such as 'The Sutton'. Broad beans prefer a sunny position and fertile, well-drained soil.

When to start

Seeds can be sown in autumn to produce a crop that will overwinter and be ready for harvesting in early summer. If your ground becomes waterlogged over winter, it's best to avoid sowing at this time as the seeds are likely to rot – sow between February and April instead. Make sure you pick a variety that suits the time of year in which you intend to sow. Ready-grown seedlings raised in cell packs are now quite widely available from garden centres or even DIY stores in early spring. These can be planted straight into the ground during March and April.

How to sow seeds

To sow outdoors, directly into the ground, prepare the soil by digging it over and removing any weeds and stones, then rake it to leave a fine finish. Sow seeds in rows in trenches 5cm (2in) deep, spacing seeds 23cm (9in) apart. Water well after covering with soil. If you intend to sow more than one row, space them 60cm (2ft) apart. As a safeguard against any seeds not germinating, sow a few extra at the end of each row that can be lifted and replanted if necessary.

If you want to grow plants in containers, sow seeds between February and April. Fill a 30–45cm (12–18in) wide container with a loam-based compost and make 5cm (2in) holes with a dibber every 10cm (4in). Drop a seed into each hole, cover with compost and water well.

Planting into the ground

Young plants bought in pots or cell packs can be planted directly into the soil in spring. Space them 23cm (9in) apart with 60cm (2ft) between rows.

How to grow

Keep plants well watered, especially when pods appear and in periods of dry weather. Pinch out the growing tips of each plant as pods begin to develop to encourage them to produce more beans. Some plants will become laden with pods and will need supporting with string attached to canes to prevent them toppling over. With care, you should be harvesting beans 12 weeks after sowing – to test them for ripeness, open a pod. Alternatively, if the beans are the size of your fingernail, they're ready.

If you are growing 'The Sutton' in pots, push a few pea sticks into the compost to provide support when plants are about 10cm (4in) tall.

What can go wrong?

Blackfly and other aphids are the pests that are most likely to trouble broad beans. Remembering to pinch out the growing tips of plants helps, as it is these young leaves that the aphids like the best. If the pest is still a problem, spray with an organic pesticide.

Pea and bean weevil damage is often noticeable as tiny round notches taken out around the edge of leaves. Although it looks unsightly, it rarely affects the harvest.

Varieties to try

'The Sutton' is an old reliable variety that can be sown in

November – it is shorter than most, so it shouldn't require any support. 'Aquadulce Claudia' can be sown in autumn or mid-winter. Broad beans are not the most attractive of crops, but 'Crimson Flowered' is an exception, with attractive red blooms. It can be sown in winter or early spring.

Carrots

Visit the supermarket and you may come across two or three different types of carrots, but dip into a seed catalogue and you'll find dozens of varieties; from short and round-rooted carrots, to those that are long and tapering. If you like unusual crops you can also order carrots that are strikingly coloured. When growing carrots be aware that they are divided into two groups: early carrots are sown in spring, while maincrop carrots are sown from April to June.

Where to grow

Carrots grow best in light, free-draining soils that contain hardly any stones. An allotment, a vegetable patch or raised bed that basks in the sun is ideal. They can be grown in pots, but if you do this choose baby or short-rooted carrots.

When to start

Seeds of early carrots can be sown in March, but will need protecting with a cloche or horticultural fleece. Maincrop carrots can be sown directly into the soil, with no protection, from April to mid-summer.

How to sow seeds

Carrot seeds need to be sown in their final position, because, being root vegetables, they need to establish themselves and do not like to be moved.

When sowing into the ground, prepare the soil well by digging it over and removing weeds and large stones, then rake it to a fine finish. Make a shallow trench, 1cm (½in) deep, with the corner of a rake and sow seeds fairly thinly. After they have germinated, thin out the row to leave carrots 8cm (3in) apart. Subsequent rows should be spaced 30cm (12in) apart.

When growing carrots in pots, sow seeds into large pots filled with loam-based compost. Either scatter the seed thinly over the surface and cover with 1cm (½in) compost or sow in short rows.

Right **Sow carrot seeds thinly in a 1cm deep trench.**
Far right **Thin seedlings to leave carrots 8cm apart.**

How to grow

Keep plants well watered to prevent the roots splitting and remove any weeds that pop up. Early varieties will be ready to pick about seven weeks after sowing, while maincrop carrots can take almost three months to reach maturity.

What can go wrong?

Carrot fly is the major pest of this crop. The fly can be attracted by the smell released when carrots are being thinned and will lay eggs that hatch into maggots and burrow into the roots. To avoid the pest, sow lightly to avoid having to thin out seedlings too much. You can also cover

the crop with fine mesh to prevent adult flies getting to them, or try sowing a carrot-fly resistant variety such as 'Flyaway', 'Sytan' or 'Resistafly'.

Varieties to try

The best carrots for pots, growing bags or window boxes include spherical 'Parmex' or finger-sized 'Mignon', both of which are good for early cropping.

For growing in the ground, 'Early Nantes 2' is a longer variety for sowing early, while 'Autumn King 2' can be sown later. For something a little different, try 'Purple Haze', which has purple skin and orange flesh, or 'Yellowstone', an interesting egg-yolk yellow colour.

Chilli peppers/sweet peppers

Whether you're a 'chilli head' or prefer the milder taste of sweet peppers, these vegetables are among the most ornamental you can grow. From mid to late summer the bushy plants literally drip with red, green, orange or even purple fruit, which dangles from the branches like the most colourful pair of barmaid's earrings.

Where to grow

For a substantial crop you can grow peppers in rows on an allotment or in a vegetable patch, but even a single plant, grown well can be incredibly productive. This makes peppers ideal for growing in raised beds, growing bags or large pots. They love a sunny, sheltered position.

When to start

Raising peppers from seed is foolproof, as it is rare for any not to germinate. They should be sown indoors from February to April – early sowings will usually result in earlier fruit. Young plants are available in late spring and you can even buy quite substantial plants already laden with fruit. These may look good, and have fruit that is ready for picking, but could you live with the guilt of knowing that you didn't do anything to raise the plant yourself?

How to sow seeds

Scatter a few seeds across the surface of an 8cm (3in) pot filled with seed compost. Sow only one or two seeds more than the number of plants you want, to compensate for any losses, as most will germinate. Cover with a fine layer of vermiculite and water. It's a good idea to put a label in the pot with the plant's name on, especially if you are sowing several varieties. Either put the pot into a heated propagator or place a clear plastic bag over the top and hold it in place with an elastic band. Position the pots in a bright, sunny spot indoors.

After the seeds have germinated, remove the pots from the propagator or remove the bag. Keep the seedlings damp but not overly wet. When they are 2cm (¾in) tall, move each seedlings into its own 8cm (3in) pot. To do this, break the rootball apart gently, hold the true leaves of the seedling and lever it up using a dibblet. Make a hole in the centre of the new pot and lower the seedling in, making sure the roots are all covered and the leaves are just above the surface of the compost. Firm in, water well and place the pot in a light spot indoors.

When roots begin to show through the bottom of the pots, transplant again into 12cm (5in) pots filled with multi-purpose compost. When plants are about 20cm (8in) tall, or before if they start to lean over, stake them with a small cane and tie up the main stem. Pinch out the tops of pepper plants when they are about 30cm (12in) tall to encourage branching.

After turning red, peppers are ready for picking.

How to grow

When the danger of frost has passed, the peppers can be moved outside. This will usually be in late May or early summer, depending on where you live in the country and what your local climate is like. However, before moving them outside permanently, you should acclimatize your seedlings to their new, cooler environment by using a technique called 'hardening off'. To do this, a week or so before you want to plant them, move the plants outside during the day and then bring them back indoors at night. Alternatively place them in a cold frame during the day and remember to close the lid at night.

Once they have got used to the cooler temperatures outdoors, you can plant them out into the ground, spaced 45cm (18in) apart, or transfer them to growing bags or larger, 23cm (9in) pots. At this stage you could also swap the small cane for a larger stake – a 90cm (3ft) cane should suffice.

Peppers are incredibly thirsty and hungry. Water regularly, being extra vigilant in hot weather and never allow compost to dry out, or this could lead to a check in growth. Feeding should start when the first flowers appear – usually while the plants are still indoors. A fortnightly dose of a liquid feed high in potash, such as tomato feed, is ideal.

The fruit will generally be ready for picking from July until September, and can be removed from plants with a sharp knife or secateurs. Plants in pots that are still bearing fruit should be put in a greenhouse or on a bright windowsill before the first frosts arrive. Those plants in the ground can be lifted and hung upside down by their roots indoors to allow the fruit to ripen.

What can go wrong?

Not too much. Greenfly or other aphids can be a problem on the shoots of young plants early in the season, but these can be rubbed off by hand if spotted early enough, or controlled with an organic pesticide if they appear in greater numbers. Plants need plenty of sunshine in order to crop well and harvests can be disappointing in poor summers.

Varieties to try

Selecting which sweet and chilli peppers to grow is a joy, as there are so many worth finding room for. You'll find 20 or so in most general seed catalogues and many, many more if you peruse those offered by a specialist supplier – some have long lists of chilli peppers. Of the sweet peppers, 'Tasty Grill Yellow' has very long yellow fruit and 'Big

Banana' has similar-shaped red fruit. 'Jumbo Sweet' is a traditionally-shaped bell pepper with extra large fruit and 'Bell Boy' has green fruit.

Choose chilli peppers based on their heat. 'Jalapeno' is fairly hot and has green fruit that turns red if it is left on the plant. 'Tabasco' is very hot, while 'Pinocchio's Nose' will blow your head off.

Courgettes

Courgettes are among the most productive vegetables in the garden. Each plant will produce masses of fruit that can be eaten throughout the summer. Unless you're feeding a huge family or like to eat courgettes at every meal, a single plant is usually enough. You might think courgettes are just sausage-shaped and green, but it is a remarkably diverse family and fruit can be yellow, striped, pale green or shaped like a tennis ball.

Where to grow

Vigorous courgettes are ideal on a sunny allotment, vegetable patch or anywhere else where the branches can be allowed to spread without getting under your feet or invading other parts of the garden. Compact or climbing varieties are perfect in growing bags or large pots, making them ideal for patios or even on a warm, sheltered balcony.

When to start

Plants can be raised from seeds that are sown in pots indoors from March to the end of May. They will be ready for planting outdoors in early summer, when there is little risk from frost, and the plants will quickly establish in warm soil. Alternatively, buy ready-grown plants or plugs for planting out in early summer, or try sowing directly into the soil outdoors at this time.

How to sow seeds

As most seeds germinate and you shouldn't need too many plants, there's no need to sow too many seeds. Start by filling an 8cm (3in) pot with compost and firm the soil down gently. Sow two seeds on their side, 2.5cm (1in) deep and cover. Put it in a heated propagator or place a clear plastic bag over the plant and hold it in place with an elastic band. Place the pot on a windowsill. When the seeds germinate, remove the weaker of the two, then, when roots begin to show through the bottom of the pot, transfer it into a 12cm (5in) container. Either plant directly into the ground outside, 60–90cm (2–3ft) apart, or into a 30–45cm (12–18in) pot filled with multi-purpose compost.

Seeds can also be sown directly into the soil in early summer. Choose a sunny, sheltered spot and dig in some well-rotted manure or compost. Sow two seeds on their side 2.5cm (1in) deep and 45–90cm (18in–3ft) apart in the row. Once germinated, hoick out the less vigorous of the two.

Harvest courgettes regularly to keep plants productive.

How to grow

As soon as the first flowers appear on the plants you need to ensure they are kept well watered and are never allowed to dry out, or else the fruits will fail to swell. If you are growing courgettes in sandy soil or in pots, apply a liquid feed that is high in potash once a week to boost the production of fruit. To keep plants productive, you need to harvest courgettes regularly to allow more fruits to develop – at the height of summer this might be about three times a week. Harvest fruit from June all the way through to mid-autumn by removing them from the plant with a sharp knife. If you are growing a climbing variety, tie the leading shoot to supports at regular intervals to prevent it bowing under the weight of the fruit and snapping.

What can go wrong?

Leaves of young plants are vulnerable to slugs and snails, and seedlings can be lost altogether. Protect plants at this early stage and, as the plants mature, they will become more able to withstand slug damage. Fruit is also vulnerable and the skin can have bites gnawed out of it by grazing slugs. Plants in pots are easy to protect, but you will need to be vigilant to keep molluscs from plants in the ground.

The disease you are most likely to come up against is powdery mildew, a fungal infection that can be detected by the powdery white coating on the upper and sometimes lower surface of leaves, especially in early autumn, which leads to loss of vigour. Remove any infected leaves that you find, then water and feed the plants well to keep them growing strongly.

Varieties to try

'Defender' has long been one of the most popular varieties of courgette, and for good reason. This is an extremely prolific variety, producing heavy crops of uniform, dark green fruit throughout the summer. If you're looking for something a bit different, 'Orelia' is an attractive, yellow-skinned courgette; 'Dario' has dark and light green stripes and looks like a slender marrow; 'Rondo di Nizza' is a round, green, Italian variety; and 'One Ball' has spherical yellow fruit. 'Midnight' is less vigorous than most and makes a compact plant for a large pot, while 'Black Forest' is perfect for really confined spaces as it can grown in a container and be trained vertically up a cane so it doesn't rob you of any valuable floor space, which you can then use for other crops if you choose.

Kale

Generations of children have greeted the arrival of kale on their school dinner plate with dismay, but this vegetable has become rather fashionable in recent years. It's also a doddle to grow. After planting out in spring or summer, plants can be left in the ground to providing pickings all the way through to the middle of spring.

Where to grow

Some varieties of kale grow quite large, so they are most suitable for growing in rows on the allotment or in a large vegetable patch or kitchen garden. However, if you're content not to have a glut, single plants can be grown in large pots or raised beds. Kale with attractive leaves are perfect for plugging gaps in beds or borders, but don't expect to be picking masses of leaves as they need plenty of space around them to fully develop – something they are unlikely to find in a traditional garden of flowers.

When to start

Kale seeds can be sown from April to June into pots indoors which can be planted out from late spring to mid-summer. If

you don't want to sow from seed, then plug plants can be
bought in spring ready for planting.

How to sow seeds

Start seeds off indoors. Fill a pot with compost and sow seeds
thinly across the surface. Cover with 2cm (¾in) of compost
then water well. The seeds should germinate within seven
days. When the seedlings are large enough to handle, 5–8
weeks from sowing, move individual plants into small pots
using a dibblet. As you do this, keep as much compost on
the roots as you can and try to avoid disturbing the plants.

Planting

Plants are ready to go outdoors from June onwards.

Planting into raised beds and pots

Plant kale into raised beds from June. If you have a small
garden and want to grow it in pots, plant it in the centre of a
45cm (18in) diameter pot filled with John Innes No 2 compost.

Planting into the ground

To ensure that individual plants have plenty of space to
grow, space them 45cm (18in) apart in a vegetable patch,

Kale is a good crop for picking in winter.

with 45cm (18in) between rows. Firm in place by pressing down with your fingertips so the seeds make good contact with the soil.

How to grow

This is really easy: keep plants well watered, especially over summer, and remove any weeds that appear. As kale grows taller, check plants regularly and re-firm them in the ground if they have been loosened by wind. Harvest later in the year by cutting complete leaves off at the base from around the outside of plants.

What can go wrong?

Kale can usually be grown without any trouble at all, though as a brassica they are potentially at risk from clubroot. This disease creates a bulbous base at the bottom of each plant; the plant's growth will be stunted and it may even die. There's no cure for clubroot and it can stay in the soil for many years, so the best way to avoid it is to prevent it by following a crop-rotation programme. Caterpillars can sometimes be a nuisance, so pick off any you spot or take the precaution of covering plants with a sheet of fine mesh. If you grow kale among perennials in the border you may find slugs and snails eat the leaves (*see page 183*).

Varieties to try

Several types of kale are real head turners, perfect for adding interest in the garden as well as on the plate. 'Black Tuscany' (cavolo nero) boasts a mass of narrow, dark green leaves that are deeply crinkled and makes a statuesque, upright plant about 1m (40in) tall. 'Red Curled' has tightly curled red leaves, 'Scarlet' has deep crimson leaves and 'Redbor' has frilly green leaves with red veins. At the lower end of the height scale is 'Dwarf Green Curled', which is good on windswept sites or even on wet soils.

Lettuces

Over the summer lettuces become a staple part of our diet, so it makes sense to save some money and grow them yourself. Ideal in any garden, they are fairly quick to get going and, despite requiring some attention, they are also quite easy to grow.

Where to grow

The wide variety of lettuces that are available in all different shapes and sizes means they are a crop that anybody can grow, whatever the size of your garden. They can be grown anywhere, and are perfect for the allotment, a vegetable patch, raised beds, containers, growing bags and window boxes. If they get too hot in summer they have a tendency to bolt, so a spot in partial shade is ideal.

When to start

Seeds can be sown directly into the soil in spring for a crop that is ready in summer. Rather than growing lots at once, which will often result in a glut, sow a short row every few weeks for a succession of lettuces to pick right through until the autumn months. Once you get the hang of sowing in

spring, you can also sow winter-hardy varieties in the autumn, which will need protecting from the elements with a cloche.

How to sow seeds

Sow seeds directly into a prepared seed bed. Make a shallow trench, 1cm (½in) deep, and sow seeds thinly along the base. Cover with soil and water well. After the seeds have germinated, thin them out – the distance between plants will depend on the variety you grow, but it is usually around 10–30cm (4–12in).

How to grow

Keep plants well watered, especially during warm, dry periods, and remove any weeds that appear. Lettuces should be harvested when mature, rather than when they are still developing. Test them by pressing the top of the plant gently to see if you can feel a firm heart. Judge whether a loose-leaf lettuce is ready to cut by how it looks. Harvest hearting lettuces by cutting them off at the base with a sharp knife.

Many lettuces have ornamental good looks.

What can go wrong?

Take precautions against slugs and snails (*see page 183*), and rub off any aphids with your fingers – if an infestation takes hold, spray with an organic pesticide. Plants can bolt or try to flower prematurely if the soil is dry, so ensure they are watered regularly.

Varieties to try

Where space is tight go for 'Little Gem' or 'Tom Thumb', both of which make compact little lettuces. 'Saladin' is a delicious iceberg type and 'Webb's Wonderful' is another popular crispy variety. 'Belize' is a bright green, oak-leaf lettuce and 'Lollo Rosso' has deep red, frilly leaves.

Onions

Onions are kitchen staple, but rather than stick to the same old varieties that are available week in, week out in the supermarket, why not grow your own and try some delicious gourmet varieties while you are at it? Once planted, the crop is easy to look after and requires very little of your time or effort.

Where to grow

You need space to grow onions, so plant them on the allotment, in a kitchen garden or a vegetable patch. They like a sunny position and well-drained soil that has had well-rotted manure dug into it the autumn before planting.

When to start

Onions are grown from sets, which are essentially small onions that can be planted straight into the ground between mid-March and mid-April. Although you can grow onions from seed, it's much tricker and isn't really worth the bother.

How to plant

Plant sets outside in a seed bed. Use a string and canes to make a straight line, then use a dibber to make holes 2.5cm (1in) deep. Drop an onion bulb into each, ensuring that the pointy end is facing upwards. Cover with soil, allowing the tip of each bulb to show above the surface, firm the soil down with your fingertips and water well.

How to grow

This bit is simple. Remove any weeds around the plants and water regularly, especially during dry weather. Bulbs are ready for harvesting in late summer when the foliage turns yellow and collapses. When this happens, lift them carefully out of the soil and allow them to dry for up to three weeks in a light place to prevent them sprouting.

What can go wrong?

Plants can sometimes bolt or run to seed prematurely, so nip out any flower shoots that appear and make sure they are kept moist in dry weather. Plants can be affected by various fungal diseases, such as downy mildew. If leaves start to get

Growing onions from sets

1 Planting sets
Place individual bulbs into holes made in a modular tray filled with compost.

2 Watering your bulbs
Leave the tips of each bulb clear of the compost and water. Avoid flooding the compost.

covered with a greyish mould, spray them with a suitable fungicide, such as one containing mancozeb.

Varieties to try

'Red Baron' has red-rimmed flesh and a strong flavour, 'Rossa lunga di Firenze' is a sweet, torpedo-shaped red onion, while 'Sturon' is an old favourite, producing good-sized bulbs that are great for storing. 'Hercules' has large round bulbs that keep well and 'Stuttgarter Giant' produces flattish-shaped onions.

3 Maintaining the crop
Place the tray in a light, cool spot and keep the compost moist, but not wet.

4 Planting
Plant individual rooted plugs 10cm (4in) apart in well prepared soil.

Potatoes

Plunging a fork into the ground and prising it upwards to reveal lots of colourful tubers is an exciting experience and one that almost requires you to shout 'eureka', especially if the potatoes are bright yellow and resemble nuggets of gold. Although the crop requires a bit of attention, growing them is easy. The hardest part is deciding what to grow in the first place, as seed catalogues are full of amazing varieties from the unusually shaped or strikingly coloured heritage potatoes, to modern varieties bred for disease resistance.

There are a lot of technical terms associated with growing potatoes, but don't let this put you off. For instance, they are categorized by the season in which they are harvested. If your potatoes are described as earlies or new potatoes, they are planted in early spring and are ready to harvest later in the same season. Maincrop potatoes need a longer period to mature – they are planted in early spring and will be ready for unearthing in late summer or early autumn.

Where to grow

Potatoes are suitable for an allotment, a vegetable garden or a raised bed and prefer fertile, well-drained soil in sun.

Salad or early varieties can be grown in large pots, hessian sacks lined with plastic, or in special growing bags that have handles to make them easy to move about if necessary.

When to start

Potatoes are not grown from seeds, but from seed potatoes – essentially tubers that are bought in late winter and can be planted in spring after they have formed sprouts. Seed potatoes are available from garden centres, nurseries, DIY stores and from mail-order suppliers. Microplants are vigorous young plants that are available from some mail-order nurseries ready for planting out in spring. Potatoes will provide a crop from May to October, depending on what you are growing and where in the country they are being grown.

Chitting potatoes

Before you plant seed potatoes you need to encourage shoots to grow, as potatoes planted directly into the soil without sprouts are unlikely to produce a worthwhile crop. This technique is known as 'chitting'. To do this, take an egg carton, a shallow cardboard box, wooden fruit tray or plastic seed tray lined with newspaper and place each potato with the rose end (the end containing most eyes) uppermost, as the sprouts will grow from these indentations. Place the carton in a cool, light spot, such as a spare room or cold porch and leave until short stubby sprouts, about 3cm (1¼in) long, have formed. This could take up to six weeks. Avoid putting potatoes in a warm, dark room as this will result in shoots being thin, long, white and spindly, like the ones you find on potatoes left at the back of a cupboard and forgotten. Shoots like this are most likely to snap off when planted.

How to plant

When the seed potatoes have formed their stubby sprouts, it's time to plant them outside.

Planting into the ground

Prepare the soil for sowing then make a wide drill about 15cm (6in) deep. Place the potatoes along the base, with the part with most stubby shoots uppermost. If you are planting first earlies these need to be about 30cm (12in) apart with 60cm (2ft) between rows; second earlies and maincrop varieties should be about 45cm (18in) apart, with 75cm (30in) between rows. Draw some soil over and water in well.

Place potatoes in the ground carefully to avoid snapping delicate sprouts.

Planting into pots

To plant, add a 10cm (4in) layer of compost to your container and roughly flatten it with your hand. Then arrange three to five tubers on top, ensuring that they are spaced evenly. Cover with another 10cm (4in) layer of compost and water.

How to grow

Potatoes growing in the ground need to be watered well, especially in periods of dry weather. When the crop reaches

Growing potatoes in a bag

1 Preparing a bag
Potatoes can be grown in strong plastic bin liners. Start by piercing a few drainage holes in the base.

2 Getting ready to plant
Fold the sides of the bag down and place a 10cm (4in) layer of compost in the bottom. Add five sprouted tubers.

3 Covering the potatoes
Cover the old potatoes with another 10cm (4in) layer of compost.

4 Watering the crop
Water the compost. When the foliage reaches 23cm (9in), cover with more compost, leaving about 8cm (3in) clear.

about 23cm (9in) tall, use a rake to draw soil around the foliage, leaving about 8cm (3in) of it clear of soil – this is a process known as earthing up. You may need to do this again if the crop puts on lots more growth.

Plants in pots need similar care. As the plants grow they will produce loads of green foliage. To prevent the developing tubers becoming green and inedible you will need to cover the foliage with compost. When plants are about 23cm (9in) tall, cover half the plant with compost and repeat this whenever necessary, stopping when you are about 10cm (4in) away from the top of the pot.

Earlies are ready for lifting once they are the size of hens' eggs. To check, scrape away the soil when the flowers drop.

What can go wrong?

The disease that every potato grower will encounter at some point is blight. This fungal disease becomes evident when the edges of leaves start to brown, and eventually leads to all foliage withering. The potatoes themselves can become discoloured before rotting. It is most likely to occur at the end of summer, during hot wet weather. Prevention is the best cure, so if the weather is wet in midsummer, spray with a copper-based fungicide, such as Bordeaux mixture.

Varieties to try

Choosing which potatoes to grow largely depends on how
you like to eat them. Potatoes with a floury texture are good
for mashing, roasting and baking, while waxy-fleshed
potatoes are better for boiling and eating in salads. Of the
first earlies, try waxy-fleshed 'Arran Pilot', all-purpose
'Kestrel' or waxy 'Charlotte'. 'Mimi' has cherry-sized,
red-skinned potatoes that are great for salads and is ideal
for growing in containers. Among the best maincrops are
red-skinned, waxy 'Desiree', knobby-shaped 'Pink Fir
Apple', which has waxy yellow flesh, and purple-skinned,
floury 'Arran Victory'.

Radishes

These crisp and peppery vegetables are the quickest and
easiest vegetables to grow. Simply sow the seed and they'll
be ready to pick a month later. Easy.

Where to grow

Radishes are happiest in sun, but they will still do well in
part shade. They can be grown in rows on the allotment,

in the vegetable garden or a raised bed, or even used to fill in gaps around other crops that take longer to mature.

When to start

Seeds can be sown from February to September, although early sowings are best covered with a cloche to provide protection from excessive cold and wet weather. Sow seeds every few weeks to ensure a continuous crop through the spring and summer.

How to sow seeds

To sow outdoors into the ground, first prepare the soil well, ensuring that its texture is like breadcrumbs. Water the soil first, allow it to soak in, then make shallow trenches, 1cm (½in) deep, with the corner of a hoe. Sow seeds thinly and cover them with soil. If you are growing several rows of radishes make sure they are 23cm (9in) apart. Seedlings will appear within 7–10 days and can be thinned out if need be.

If you want to grow radishes in pots or window boxes, choose short, round or stump-rooted varieties that do not need deep soil to thrive. Fill a large pot (30cm (12in) in diameter and 20cm (8in) deep is ideal) with multi-purpose compost. Sow seeds thinly on the surface and cover with

1cm (½in) of compost, then water well and position the pot in a sunny spot.

After removing plants from growing bags at the end of the season, you could reuse the bag by cutting out a single panel and sowing short rows of radishes along the top. At this cooler time of year, put the bag in a greenhouse or a light front porch for protection from harsh weather conditions.

How to grow

There's very little to do to keep radishes happy. Make sure the plants are well watered, especially during periods of dry weather, and remove any weeds that appear around the crop. Radishes are ready for harvesting between April and October, or even later depending on the variety.

What can go wrong?

Very little, as long as the crop is kept moist. Slugs and snails are likely to be your biggest problem, so protect plants or control as necessary (*see page 183*).

Varieties to try

'French Breakfast', 'Flamboyant Sabina' and 'Mirabeau' have long roots and are ideal for growing in the ground;

'Sparkler', 'Scarlet Globe' and 'Pink Slipper' have round or oval roots and are suitable for pots. For something more unusual, try 'Hilds blauer Herbst und Winter' – its long purple roots can be picked as late as November.

Rocket

The peppery leaves of rocket have become a staple of summer salads, but why spend money on expensive bags from the supermarket when it is so easy to grow these leaves yourself? The answer? Well, there's no good reason, so start growing your own.

Where to grow
You can grow armfuls of rocket by sowing a few rows in a sunny or even partially shaded spot on the allotment, or in the vegetable garden. If you don't have much space you could grow rocket in growing bags, pots, or even in a window box.

When to start
Seeds can be sown directly into the ground or into pots any time from March to September. You can have a regular

supply of leaves by sowing every few weeks over the growing season so you have young plants to replace those that become exhausted. For leaves to pick over autumn and winter, sow seeds under glass (a greenhouse or cold frame) between September and March. You may sometimes see plug plants of rocket for sale, but there's little point buying them as they are so easy to raise from seed, and feel much more satisfying when grown in this way.

How to sow seeds

To sow outdoors into the soil, prepare the ground well before sowing by digging it over and removing weeds and large stones. Rake to a fine finish. To sow, make a shallow trench, 1cm (½in) deep, with the corner of the rake. Sow seeds thinly in the base, cover and water. Once the seeds have germinated, thin out seedlings so they are roughly 15cm (6in) apart.

To grow in pots filled with multi-purpose compost, you have two choices that will both lead to roughly the same result. Either scatter seeds thinly across the surface of your chosen container and cover with 1cm (½in) compost, or sow in rows, 1cm (½in) deep and cover. Firm the soil gently and water well.

How to grow

There's nothing to it. Water regularly to prevent the soil or compost drying out and pick leaves regularly from the outside of plants to ensure they produce lots more leaves from the centre. Remove any weeds that try to muscle in among the plants.

What can go wrong?

Cabbage white butterflies may try to lay their eggs on rocket, so remove any caterpillars that appear. If you are

Pick leaves from around the outside to encourage more to grow from the centre.

growing lots of plants in the ground you could prevent butterflies from reaching the crop by covering plants with fine mesh. Plants will eventually bolt or run to seed, but this process can be accelerated if plants are under stress because of dry roots. Prevent this happening by keeping on top of the watering to make sure your plants have plenty to drink.

Varieties to try

There aren't too many. Cultivated rocket (*Eruca vesicaria*) and rocket (*Eruca sativa*) have oval leaves with a strong flavour. Wild rocket has frilly leaves and a more pungent taste. The variety 'Skyrocket' combines the taste and looks of wild rocket with the growing speed of rocket.

Runner beans

Freshly picked runner beans are a real treat and are far tastier than those you can pick up from the supermarket. They are also an excellent vegetable for beginner gardeners to tackle, as you can reap a bumper harvest for the minimum of effort on your part.

Where to grow

Runner beans are ideal for growing in a sunny space on the allotment or in a vegetable bed where there is room to set up a supporting structure for this climbing plant. These beans can also be grown in very large pots, as long as there is room in the container to make a wigwam of canes. Alternatively, try a compact runner bean, such as 'Hestia', that doesn't need such robust supports and can even be grown in sheltered window boxes.

When to start

Sow seeds in pots indoors in mid-April for planting outdoors between mid-May and June. Seeds can also be sown directly into the ground between mid-May and June. Your garden centre may have rooted seedlings grown in cell trays that are available for sale and can be planted straight into the ground in late spring or early summer.

How to sow seeds

Runner bean seeds should be sown into well-prepared, fertile soil that has had plenty of manure dug into it the previous autumn. Before sowing, though, set up your supports. The traditional method is to erect two rows of

slanted canes that are held together by a cross bar running across the middle. To do this, make two straight lines, 60cm (2ft) apart. Push in 2.5m (8ft) long canes, 30cm (12in) apart, along the first row then repeat this on the second row, making sure they are directly opposite. Now angle the canes towards each other until they just overlap to make a triangle. Use another cane as a crossbar and tie together. You may need an extra pair of hands to do this. Alternatively, if you only want to grow a few beans or have a raised bed, erect a wigwam of six to seven canes bound with twine.

Sow two seeds at the base of each cane 5cm (2in) deep and water them in well. After germination, remove the weakest of the two and allow the other one to climb up the cane. To help it on its way you can secure it to the cane with twine. When planting ready-grown beans, plant one at the foot of each cane and tie the growth to the supports.

How to grow

Water plants well, particularly from when the first flower buds appear until the last of the crop has been picked. When the beans reach the top of their supports, pinch out the tops

Pick beans often to prevent them turning tough and stringy.

to encourage them to make more pods and prevent them becoming too top heavy. You can expect to be picking beans about three months after sowing. Harvest them every few days to ensure a constant supply and to prevent any from becoming tough.

What can go wrong?
Aphids are the major pest that cause unsightly damage but no serious harm. The tiny greenfly or blackfly are usually found lurking on the tips of young shoots or on the undersides of leaves. As soon as you spot them, spray them with an organic pesticide or leave them for birds, ladybirds or spiders to feast on.

Varieties to try
'Enorma' is a great beginner's variety and will reward you with a prolific crop. 'St George' has bi-coloured red and white flowers, and is an improvement on the traditional 'Painted Lady'. For stringless pods try 'White Apollo' or 'Lady Di'. If space is tight, try the dwarf runner bean 'Hestia', which only grows to 45cm (18in).

Salad leaf mixtures

Blends of different leafy salads have become incredibly popular over the last few years. These are among the fastest plants you can grow and seed mixes are made up of a variety of different crops, including mustard, kale, chard, lettuce and oriental salad leaves.

Where to grow
Salad leaves can be grown in pots, window boxes, growing bags or in the vegetable garden.

When to start
Most salad leaf mixtures are suitable for sowing outdoors between March and August, and will be ready to start picking three to four weeks later. For a continuous supply of leaves, simply sow every two to three weeks. For those who like salads during cooler times of the year, try mixtures that can be grown under protection during colder months.

How to sow seeds
Either gently scatter seeds thinly across the surface of the multi-purpose compost in your chosen container then cover

with 1cm (½in) compost, or sow in rows, 1cm (½in) deep. Cover with a layer of compost, and firm the soil gently and water well.

To sow outdoors into the ground, sow seeds 1cm (½in) deep in rows 15cm (6in) apart. As the seedlings grow, thin them out so they are spaced about 3.5cm (1½in) apart and have room to develop.

How to grow

Water the plants well and pick leaves regularly to keep them productive and prevent plants going to seed. Either pick individual leaves as required or snip a whole plant off about 2.5cm (1in) above ground level – it will soon re-sprout. Most can be cut like this several times before they eventually run out of steam.

What can go wrong?

If you don't pick regularly you'll find that the strongest varieties in each mixture will try to take over. To prevent this happening you could remove varieties that are in greater abundance at the seedling stage. These are short-lived crops, so expect them to bolt (flower and set seed) a few weeks after you start picking.

A salad leaf mixture will add a vibrant touch to meals.

Varieties to try

Salad leaf mixes include different varieties to appeal to many tastes. If you like something spicy go for 'Bright and Spicy Salad Leaves' or 'Oriental Mustards'. For something milder try 'Herby Salad Mix', 'French Mix' or 'Californian Mix'. For sowing later in the year, try 'Winter Blend' or 'Niche Oriental Mixed'.

Salad onions

For an ultra-fast crop that will add a fiery kick to salads or perk up a dull stir-fry, try sowing some salad onions. This group includes spring onions and Japanese bunching onions, which are grown the same way, but have straight stems rather than stems that end in a bulb. These are some of the quickest vegetables you can grow, with a crop that is ready to harvest just 12 weeks after sowing.

Where to grow

Perfect on a sunny allotment, in a vegetable garden or in raised beds, another plus point is that they can also be grown in pots, window boxes and growing bags, in situations where space is scarce.

When to start

Sow seeds from late winter and through the summer. Seeds can also be sown in autumn for a crop that is ready to pick early the following year, however plants will need covering with cloches to survive the winter period.

Super fast spring onions are ready to pick within 12 weeks of sowing.

How to sow seeds

To sow outdoors into the soil, prepare the ground well by digging it over, removing weeds and any big stones, then raking it well to leave a fine finish. Sow seeds thinly in shallow trenches, 1cm (½in) deep, cover and water well. Subsequent rows should be 30cm (12in) apart. Some varieties don't require thinning, but with those that do remove seedlings when they are large enough to handle, leaving the onions 1cm (½in) apart.

When sowing into pots, broadcast the seeds fairly thickly in large pots filled with multi-purpose compost, or in rows across the surface of the soil, then cover with compost and water well.

How to grow

Water plants well and remove any weeds. It's best to do this by hand to avoid damaging the stems with a hoe.

What can go wrong?

Downy mildew can be a problem. If you see a white fluffy fungal growth on plants, remove those that are infected. The problem can be avoided by sowing thinly, which will allow air to circulate around the plants, and by not overwatering.

Varieties to try

If you thought a spring onion was just a spring onion, think again; there are many varieties of this humble salad vegetable. 'White Lisbon' is white skinned and mild, 'Lilia' has a red inner core, 'Crimson Forest' has red stalks, and 'Summer Isle' is a Japanese bunching onion with a sweet taste. 'Performer' is a good onion for growing all year round.

Swiss chard

Sometimes called leaf beets, Swiss chard is grown for its tasty leaves and stems that are cooked in the same way as spinach. But there the comparison with the green vegetable favoured by Popeye ends. Swiss chard is amazing to look at and is available with stems in a wide range of colours that wouldn't look out of place in flower border.

Where to grow

Their good looks mean that Swiss chard can be dotted among perennials or other plants in beds or borders, but for a larger crop grow them on the allotment or in the vegetable patch in moisture-retentive soil. Those with smaller gardens could grow plants in large pots or raised beds. In any of these situations, make sure they are given a sunny or slightly shaded spot.

When to start
Seeds can be sown from April to July directly into the soil, or you can buy plug plants that are ready for planting out.

How to sow seeds
Ensure your chard romps away by preparing the soil well. Dig it over, removing weeds and any large stones, then rake it to a fine finish. When the soil has been levelled, make a shallow trench, 2.5cm (1in) deep, with the corner of the rake and sow seeds thinly along the base. Cover with soil and water well. After they have germinated, thin out seedlings so they are about 30cm (12in) apart. If you want to sow extra rows, these should be 38cm (15in) apart. Seeds sown in spring will result in plants that can be harvested over summer, while later sowings will give a crop that can be picked into winter, as long as plants are protected with a cloche from autumn onwards.

Ruby chard can add a colourful touch to a border.

To grow chard in pots, start by filling an 8cm (3in) pot with compost, sowing seeds thinly and covering them with a 2.5cm (1in) layer of compost. When seedlings are 2.5cm (1in) tall, re-pot them into small, individual pots. The young plants can either be planted singly into 12cm (5in) diameter pots, or you can put several into a 45cm (18in) container.

How to grow

Keep plants moist and give them a boost every couple of weeks with a liquid fertilizer that is high in nitrogen. Weeds will rob chard of water and nutrients, so tug out any that appear. Leaves will be ready for picking about 12 weeks after sowing – take what you need by harvesting from the outside of the plant, cutting them off with a sharp knife. Frequent picking will ensure lots of fresh leaves grow from the centre of the plant.

What can go wrong?

Not much. This is a tough, easy-going crop. You might sometimes find slugs and snails on plants (*see page 183*), but otherwise you need only to be careful not to damage the roots when cutting the leaves away with a knife.

Varieties to try

The most striking seed mixture is 'Bright Lights', which contains chard with red, white, orange, yellow and pink stems. 'Ruby Chard' has glossy green leaves and pillarbox-red stems and veins, and 'Oriole Orange' has orange stems. 'Lucullus' has green leaves that contrast with white stems and is a more prolific version of Swiss chard, that shares similar looks.

Tomatoes

Nothing beats eating tomatoes picked straight from the vine, so it's no surprise that it is the most popular vegetable plant grown by gardeners. There's a world of difference between the home-grown version and the bland, water-filled baubles you find in most shops. Not only do tomatoes raised in the garden smell great, but the taste of fruit that has ripened naturally outdoors over a long growing season is far richer than that of the commercial crops that have been grown under glass, placed in a cold store and then ripened artificially with gasses.

Where to grow

Tomatoes are a diverse tribe of plants that are classified by their growing habit. You might sometimes see the words 'indeterminate', 'semi-determinate' or 'determinate' variety printed in small letters on the seed packet. This refers to the way that tomatoes are classified. Those grown as a single stem up a cane are described as indeterminate, or cordon, varieties, bush tomatoes are known as determinate varieties and semi-determinate varieties are bush varieties that are very vigorous and need pinching back to keep within bounds.

Vine (cordon or indeterminate) tomatoes are perfect for large pots and growing bags in the greenhouse or for growing in the ground outdoors, as long as you can provide robust supports to hold up the fruit-laden stems. Bush or determinate varieties need room to spread, so they are better saved for the vegetable patch or in a raised bed. Vigorous bush or semi-determinate varieties need even more room and require pinching back to keep them within bounds. Compact bush tomatoes are perfect in containers, window boxes or hanging baskets.

Vine tomatoes need supporting with canes.

When to start

Tomatoes can be started from seeds sown in late winter/
early spring, or bought as plugs in late spring. Plugs will
need planting into pots so they can bulk up before being
planted outdoors. Tomato plants can be moved outdoors as
soon as there is no danger from frost, usually in late May.
Larger plants bought in early summer can be planted
outdoors immediately.

How to sow seeds

Tomato seeds need to be sown under cover. Fill 8cm (3in)
pots with compost, lightly firm it down and water it. Scatter
the seeds thinly over the surface – most of them will
germinate, so only sow a few more seeds than you need
plants – and cover with a thin layer of vermiculite. Label the
pots and place them in a heated propagator to germinate (or
put a clear freezer bag over the top of the pot and secure it
with an elastic band), then place them on a light windowsill.

Seedlings should appear between 7–10 days, at which
time you should remove the propagator lid, or the plastic
bag. The seedlings will be large enough to move into
separate pots when they are about 5cm (2in) tall. To do this,
remove the rootball from the pot, put it onto a flat surface

and gently loosen the roots with a dibblet (a pencil will do). Hold a seedling carefully by its true leaves and gently lever it up with the dibblet. Make a hole in an 8cm (3in) pot filled with multi-purpose compost and carefully lower the seedling into it. Gently firm it in, making sure the roots are covered, and water well. When the roots come through the drainage holes in the pot, transplant the tomato plant into a 12cm (5in) pot. If the seedling starts to droop, support it with a pea stick, and later a cane.

Planting

Tomatoes are ready for planting outdoors when all danger of frost has passed and after a period of hardening off, which is generally when the first truss of flowers appear. Make sure you choose a warm, sunny spot to encourage plants to romp away and to ensure the fruit will ripen fully.

Planting in growing bags and pots

Prepare the bag by shaking and kneading it to break up clods of compacted compost and form into a hummock shape. Make slits in the base for drainage holes and cut out the marked planting squares. Scoop out enough compost for the root balls of the plants, then backfill with compost until the top of the root ball is beneath the top of the bag and has a light covering of compost over it. Firm in and water well. Erect a growing bag frame over the bag and insert a cane next to each plant. Secure the canes to the frame and, as the plants grow, tie them to the cane every 10cm (4in) up the height of the main stem.

Single tomato plants can be grown in 30cm (12in) containers filled with a loam-based compost. Supporting plants in pots can be difficult, so stick to bush varieties if you have no way of holding the canes in an upright position.

Planting into the ground

If you are planning on growing a number of tomatoes in the ground, make sure you give plants enough space to allow fruits to develop. Vine tomatoes growing up canes need about 45cm (18in) between them, while vigorous, spreading bush varieties should be spaced 90cm (3ft) apart.

How to grow

Bush tomatoes require very little maintenance. Simply prune back shoots if the plants are growing outside their allotted

Right **Regularly tie tomato shoots to supports with garden twine.**
Far right **Remove sideshoots from vine tomatoes with a simple snapping motion.**

area. Vine tomatoes need a bit more attention as the aim is to create a single-stemmed plant. They can become very top heavy when laden with fruit, so they need strong supports. If you are growing them in the ground, push thick canes deeply into the ground next to each plant. When using a growing bag, slip a special growing bag frame over the bag. Regularly tie the central shoot to the cane as it grows and snap off any shoots that appear in the joint between the

main stems and leaves. When your plant has produced four sets of flowering trusses, pinch out the central growing tip to ensure its energy goes into producing fruit, and not more foliage. For a bumper crop, feed plants weekly once flowers appear with a liquid tomato food that is high in potash, such as Tomorite, and ensure the soil never dries out. Indoor plants will produce ripe fruit from late July, outdoor-grown plants from August until around late September/October.

What can go wrong?

There are several pest and disease problems that affect tomatoes, but the main two you are likely to encounter are blossom end rot and blight.

Blossom end rot is often caused by irregular watering. This disease causes the base of the tomato to turn black and hard due to lack of calcium, which is found in water. To prevent this happening, water well and regularly and don't allow the compost to dry out. Be careful with your watering, as fruit can split if you overwater or in summers when there is heavy rainfall. Splitting can also occur if the soil at root level has been allowed to dry and then watered thoroughly.

Tomato blight is a problem that occurs in warm, wet summers. This fungal disease causes brown patches on the upper side of shrivelled foliage and rotting fruit. Prevent it by spraying plants with a copper-based fungicide, such as Bordeaux mixture, before fruit has set. Or grow a blight-resistant variety like 'Ferline' or 'Legend'.

Varieties to try

As there are hundreds of different varieties of tomato available, choosing what to grow can cause plenty of head scratching. The solution is to try some new varieties each year. Even if you only have room for a single growing bag, it will give you the opportunity to grow three different tomatoes. Among the best vine varieties are 'Black Russian', 'Super Marmande' and 'Ferline'. 'Tumbler' and 'Green Sausage' are excellent bush varieties, while 'Black Cherry', 'Suncherry' and 'Golden Cherry' have tasty, cherry-sized fruit. If you're looking for a plum tomato to cook with, 'Roma' is a great choice. 'Tumbling Tom Red', 'Balconi Red' and 'Hundreds and Thousands' are good for baskets and pots. If you're looking for a compact bush variety, 'Vilma' or 'Totem' are both stocky and productive.

Maintaining your vegetable garden

For a successful vegetable garden you need to spend time maintaining the crops and the ground they grow in, so that you can enjoy a bountiful harvest. While much of the work will take place during the main growing season, between spring and autumn, for thriving, productive plants there are some jobs and techniques that need to be carried out at other times of the year too.

Watering

Water is essential to prevent your crops becoming too stressed and to ensure an adequate harvest, whether you are growing them for their roots, fruits or leaves. A lack of moisture while plants are growing can cause damage to fruit, such as blossom end rot on tomatoes, or the premature running to seed (bolting) of leafy plants like lettuces. It can also result in a lack of vigour that makes plants more vulnerable and less able to cope with attacks from pests and diseases.

In a wet summer, plants in the ground should romp away with the minimum of additional watering, but it still pays to check them regularly and to water if necessary. In a dry summer plants will be extremely vulnerable, so watering once or even twice a day might be necessary. In your own garden it's easy to react quickly to the needs of your plants, but on an allotment, or where the crops are grown out of sight, you must make sure you visit your plants often.

Those who grow just a few vegetables might be able to get away with using a watering can fitted with rose, but if you have lots of plants, make life easier for yourself by using a hosepipe with a long-handled lance connected to the end.

Conserve moisture

Soil that is light and prone to drying out rapidly can be improved by digging in manure, leaf mould or garden compost (*see page 184*). This allows it to hold on to moisture more effectively, releasing it to the roots of plants when it is needed. Mulching the soil in vegetable gardens with a 5cm (2in) layer of any of the same materials you also use to dig in, will also help to lock in moisture and prevent its speedy evaporation from the surface in sunny, dry or windy weather. Keeping soil free of weeds will also help to conserve moisture, as they soak up water like a sponge, and will deprive your vegetables.

This device allows you to reach into the bed easily and to accurately direct the spray of water to just above the root zone, without eroding any soil. Ensure you give plants a good soak so the water penetrates the surface of the soil; simply wetting the soil will not allow the water to reach the roots and the soil will dry out quickly again.

Vegetables in pots are more vulnerable than those in the ground as the limited amount of compost can dry out quickly. Water any container-grown plants frequently through the summer and consider replacing watering cans or hoses with a drip-irrigation system. This can be fitted to an outdoor tap, and the programmable computerized timer will ensure that water is applied at a set time to keep plants moist. These hi-tech systems are ideal for busy or forgetful gardeners, or for when you may be away for any length of time.

Feeding

Some vegetables will grow quite adequately without feeding, but you'll get better results if you provide plants with certain nutrients to boost their growth. Most plants are in need of three major nutrients to grow: nitrogen (N), phosphorous (P) and potassium (K), which are generally referred to as NPK on fertilizer packets. Each of these three nutrients has a different effect on plants: Nitrogen encourages leafy growth, phosphorous builds a strong root system, and potassium helps with the development of flowers and fruit. To be healthy, plants also need a mixture of other nutrients, such as calcium, magnesium and iron, which are often found in smaller amounts in most general fertilizers.

There are several different types of fertilizer that can be used in the vegetable garden. Powdered feed or granules are

Tomatoes need feeding with a fertilizer high in potash.

NPK ratio

The amount of NPK included in fertilizers is written as a ratio. Many general plant feeds have an NPK ration of 15:30:15 respectively, which means it will improve the health of all parts of the plant; a feed that is high in potassium, such as liquid tomato food, might show a ratio of 6:5:9. A plant food that is high in nitrogen, which can boost crops like spinach, might have a ratio of 25:15:15.

scattered over the soil, liquid feeds can be added to water in a watering can, and controlled-release fertilizer granules can be mixed into compost for vegetables grown in containers.

Powdered feeds or granules are generally applied to the soil a few weeks before sowing, so they can release the nutrients slowly to the plants. Liquid feeds are applied every week, or every few weeks, directly to the soil or compost in pots, usually when vegetables grown for their fruit come into flower. Controlled-release fertilizer granules, which release their nutrients over a period of time, should be mixed into compost prior to potting up plants.

Other fertilizers, which contain a particular nutrient at a specific level, are applied to plants as a pick-me-up if they are suffering from a nutrient deficiency.

Pest and disease control

At some point, most gardeners have wondered why their garden, or a certain plant, has become a magnet for pests or diseases. Slugs, snails, aphids, vine weevils and other troublesome creepy crawlies, along with a whole host of unpleasant diseases, can cause carnage if unseen, but if spotted early you have a good chance of preventing a problem getting out of hand.

The key to pest and disease control is vigilance. Inspect your crops regularly by looking under leaves and on the tips of shoots, which are a delicacy for aphids. Do this on a daily basis or every other day and avoid just giving the plants a cursory glance, as you might miss something and by the time you look again you may have a trouble on your hands. Apart from physically checking your plants, give them a visual test – if they look sick, don't just leave them or assume it's down to your watering or feeding regime. Examine them carefully and look for anything else that may be causing a problem.

If your vegetables have a problem you might be able to control it by letting nature take its course – birds, hoverflies, lacewings, ladybirds and spiders feast on aphids, and birds love slugs and snails. Sometimes squashing all the pests you find is enough to stop them spreading, but if the pest population is nearing plague proportions then you may have to spray with a suitable pesticide. There are many available in garden centres and DIY stores, so check that it's suitable for tackling the specific pest that is causing a nuisance. While many sprays will contain chemicals, biological controls often contain ingredients derived from plants and are favoured by organic gardeners. What you use is up to you and whatever suits your gardening approach.

As with pests, you can sometimes curb diseases by removing infected leaves. However, you may need to spray if a disease has become advanced or, in more extreme cases, remove the plant completely from the ground and destroy it to stop the spread.

When growing vegetables you should always take steps to prevent problems occurring in the first place. For instance, if your garden or plot is a haven for slugs and snails, use some form of control after planting. Pellets can be scattered carefully around plants, following the instructions on the packet, or you can protect vulnerable plants with cloches – a DIY way of doing this is to cut sections from plastic drinks bottles to put around seedlings. If you are growing in pots or raised beds, try attaching sticky backed copper tape to the surface – slugs and snails hate to cross it. Likewise, vegetables bearing fruit or nearing the stage where they are ready to be harvested can be covered with mesh or netting to prevent flying pests from reaching and damaging the crops.

The likelihood of diseases striking or spreading from plant to plant is lessened by following the correct spacings for planting. This ensures good air movement around plants,

Far left **Sap sucking aphids can be controlled by hand if spotted early enough.**
Left **Irregular holes in leaves are a sign of slug damage.**

allowing them to grow healthily. Vegetables that are planted at the correct spacing, kept clear of weeds and regularly fed and watered, tend to be healthier than those that are crammed in and given very little aftercare. Even if they do attract the attention of pests or succumb to a disease, the vigour of plants that are grown well tends to help them shrug off problems more easily.

Composting

When you grow vegetables you will generate plenty of waste, whether it's due to crops being damaged, left overs after harvesting, or the compost that remains in pots after annual vegetables have finished. Even when the crop is picked and prepared in the kitchen, you'll have lots of empty pods, peelings or the cut-off ends from root crops to deal with. Rather than consign all of this to the wheelie bin, it's a good idea to recycle it by turning the waste into compost that can dug back into the garden to boost the soil's nutrient level, or can be spread across the surface as a mulch.

Garden waste can make perfect compost to improve your soil.

If you've got a large garden there are plenty of types of bin you can consider. Look through the catalogues sent out by horticultural companies and you'll find plenty of styles: from big square boxes made from timber to plastic domes; attractive bins in the shape of a beehive to compost tumblers. What you go for should depend on how much waste you generate, where you want to put the bin and how much money you are willing to spend. Some local councils also offer discounted compost bins to residents to encourage composting, so check with them too.

If you have a tiny garden you are unlikely to have room for a compost bin, but you can still recycle much of your vegetable waste with a compact worm bin. This is a four-tiered bin that's around 75cm (30in) high, can be easily pushed into a vacant corner and won't stick out like a sore thumb. It is a brilliant system that relies on an army of worms to do all the hard work – all you have to do is add vegetable peelings, shredded newspaper, used tea bags, flower heads and coffee grounds to the trays and the worms will make their way through it, turning the waste into a lovely rich compost.

Apart from garden waste, it's a good idea to collect fallen leaves in autumn to turn into leafmould, which is a lovely material that will improve your soil. If you have the space, you could build a dedicated bin in which to store your leaves.

Building a leaf bin

To do this, make a cage-like structure with four 1.2m (4ft) tree stakes, a roll of galvanized chicken wire, ten galvanized U-staples, a mallet, a hammer and a pair of wire clippers. Choose a spot on soil or grass, as this will encourage worms into the leaves and allow excess moisture to drain away. Hammer the stakes into the ground, 60cm (2ft) apart, to make a square shape. Keep the stakes as upright as possible, allowing about 90cm (3ft) of each to remain above the ground. Secure the end of the chicken wire to the first post with two U-staples. Then unroll the mesh to the next post, secure it with staples and repeat until you have a square enclosure. Finish by snipping off excess wire with the clippers and bend in any dangerous ends of wire that might be sticking out.

If you don't have the space for a leaf bin, or only have a small garden that doesn't generate many leaves, collect them in black plastic bin liners and puncture some holes in the base and sides of the bag. This will aid drainage, allow air to enter and prevent the contents turning slimy. When

Leaf stored in bags will turn to leafmould within two years.

the bag is almost full, sprinkle the leaves with a little water, give the bag a shake and tie it up. When you open the bag in a year's time the material will be fairly coarse and can be used as a mulch; leave it for another year and it will rot down even further. Leafmould is an excellent soil fertilizer, containing high levels of humus, which can be dug into the ground to help soil retain moisture and hold on to nutrients.

Attracting wildlife

Many of us like to attract wildlife into the garden because it makes it a far more interesting place to spend time, but if that's not a good enough reason for you, maybe this is: having a garden that literally buzzes with life helps to naturally control pests that like to chomp on your vegetables, so you don't have to resort to chemical controls.

Hedgehogs, birds, beetles, frogs, toads, lacewings, ladybirds and many other creatures that visit the garden devour nasty bugs, so it is really worthwhile thinking of ways to attract them and keep them happy.

Perhaps the best time to start turning your space into a back-garden nature reserve is in the autumn, when the leaves are starting to fall. Abandon all plans of a traditional tidy up at this time as too much cleaning can be detrimental. Many creatures are starting to hibernate and waking them up can mean you will have fewer natural predators to take on pests in the spring, while rousing larger creatures will cause them distress and place demands on their already depleted reserves of fat. All of this means there is less likelihood that the predators will survive the winter.

Among the garden good guys that like to bed down for the winter are slug-eating frogs, toads and hedgehogs, some butterflies, spiders and ladybirds. When you consider that just a single one of these distinctive red-and-black spotted insects can eat around 2000 aphids in its lifetime, you really don't need a better excuse to steer clear of excessive tidying. As ladybirds and other creatures like to hibernate in hollow stems, avoid razing all your perennials to ground level unless absolutely necessary. Most plants can be happily left until spring, when you can chop them back before new growth appears. It also pays to leave piles of leaves or twigs in the garden as they may be sheltering newts, frogs, toads or hedgehogs.

Right **Pollinating insects are important for flowering vegetables.**
Far right **Frogs have a ravenous appetite for slugs.**

If you have a shed or greenhouse, don't feel you have to organize it or sweep it every time you happen to have time on your hands. Many creatures, such as lacewings and butterflies, tuck themselves away in the nooks and crannies of garden buildings, or they might hide themselves under pots or behind bags of compost.

Of course, you will also need to help wildlife that remains active over the winter. Birds are extremely vulnerable during cold snaps, when they often have trouble finding

natural food. To help them survive the winter months, put out bird feeders filled with high-energy food that is full of calories, such as peanuts and sunflower seeds.

Remember to leave out plenty of fresh water in a shallow dish so they have somewhere to clean their feathers and have a drink – this is essential when you put out dry food and natural water reserves may be frozen over. Top up the water on a regular basis and break up the ice if it has frozen over.

If you have an allotment, try taking a closer look at an uncultivated or abandoned area that is choked by a mass of brambles. Okay, it may look messy, but it also supports a diverse population of wildlife. So, be inspired and rather than keeping all of the grass around your plot cut short, choose a patch that is out of the way and let it grow naturally. Ladybirds will soon discover it and use it as a place to hibernate over winter, and will reward you in return by feasting on aphids.

Many allotments are surrounded by trees, which yield lots of dead branches. Instead of burning all of this material, gather it up and make a log pile. All you need to do is

A bug box makes an ideal hibernation home for many beneficial insects.

arrange a few pieces randomly and let them rot down naturally. Put it in a shady spot under a tree, beneath a hedge or around the back of a shed and frogs, toads, beetles and hedgehogs will all use it as a shelter.

Elsewhere, prune hedges and fruit trees later in the winter rather than in autumn as these are a source of food and shelter for many creatures, and leave fallen fruit on the ground for the birds. It's also a good idea to avoid disturbing your compost heap too much over winter. Many insects, mammals and creatures like to use them to hibernate in.

Improving your soil

Apart from adding fertilizers to the soil, it is also a good idea to enrich it before planting by adding plenty of organic matter, such as leafmould, garden compost or well-rotted manure. Not only will this boost the nutrient content of the soil, but it will improve its structure and help it to retain moisture. To do this, spread a 5cm (2in) layer of the material over the soil and fork it into the surface to a depth of about 10cm (4in). To give existing beds a boost, mulch around plants with organic matter in the spring.

Mulches

Vegetable beds can dry out surprisingly quickly in sunny spells or be taken over by weeds, which can lead to plant growth being checked and can put extra pressure on you to provide water, or to grab the hoe and carry out some emergency weeding.

A great solution to this problem is to mulch beds or individual plants. Covering the surface with a layer of material can help to provide nutrients to plants, it locks in moisture, forms a barrier to prevent weeds from germinating, and helps to insulate the roots of perennials from the winter cold.

In spring, after watering apply a 5cm (2in) layer of garden compost, well-rotted manure or leafmould as a ring around newly planted annual vegetables. It is important that the ground is already moist, as it's harder to wet the soil with the mulch in place. The mulch will act a sealing layer to hold the moisture in place in the soil, while also preventing loss of water by evaporation. A layer of mulch can also be added to perennial vegetables, but this should be carried out in early spring while the soil is still damp, but is also starting to warm up after winter. Be sure to leave a gap between the mulch and the stems of the vegetables to prevent rotting.

Mulching large areas

On allotments, or other large areas, lay down mulch to prevent weeds from growing on parts of the land you haven't got round to planting up. Lengths of old carpet laid across the soil are ideal for this – you may find pieces abandoned in the hedges around your allotment or be able to rescue a roll that has been dumped in a skip.

Alternatively, you can buy a roll of landscape material from a DIY store or garden centre. The black material can be rolled over the soil surface and held down with pegs or bricks to prevent it flapping in the breeze. Although the sheeting prevents light from reaching the surface, which has the advantage of stifling the growth of weeds, it is semi-permeable so it still allows rain to pass through. You can then roll back the sheeting as your plants progress across the bed.

In the autumn, you may wish to mulch vegetable beds with well-rotted farmyard manure. Do this to a light, well-drained soil that has been dug over well. Completely cover with a 5cm (2in) layer of mulch, then cover it with landscape material and leave it over winter. When you remove the cover in spring, most of the manure will have been taken into the soil by worms and any that is still sitting on the surface can be dug in.

Garden compost makes a great mulch for vegetables.

Green manure

Green manure is a term used to describe a number of fast-growing plants that are grown on bare soil, usually over the winter period. Green manures are ideal for larger spaces, such as allotments or vegetable gardens, and have many benefits. The foliage of these plants provides ground cover to smother weeds and at the same time prevents loss of nutrients from the soil by winter rain. In spring, you can dig the plants back into the ground while they are still green. By doing so you will release their valuable nutrients back into the soil and they will act like organic matter, making the soil easier to work. The plants can also provide shelter and places for beneficial creatures to hibernate over the cold winter months.

Green manures are most often sown in the autumn, after crops have been harvested and the plants removed. Among those that can be sown at this time are winter grazing rye, which can be dug into the soil the following spring, and mustard, which is best sown before mid-September. Field beans and vetches can also be sown in the autumn. These have an advantage over some other green manures in that the plants belong to the pea and bean family (legumes), and are able to store nitrogen in their roots. When they are dug into the soil this nutrient gives the crops that follow them a big boost.

If you have ground that lies empty at other times of the year, you could consider sowing a green manure to keep weeds down. For example, buckweed or fenugreek can be sown in summer, along with lupins, clovers and peas, which also have the benefit of all being legumes.

To grow a green manure, either sow seeds in rows across the soil or broadcast them then rake them into the surface. Before they flower, or once the land is needed for cropping, chop the foliage down and leave it to wilt. Dig the plants into the top 15cm (6in) of soil, where they will decompose and release any stored nutrients. After digging in, the site should be left for two weeks or more before sowing or planting out, as decaying foliage can harm plant growth.

Protecting crops

Crops grown in the ground are vulnerable to frost and other adverse weather conditions from autumn through to early spring, and pests can still cause problems too. Protect vegetables that are planted or sown early, or those that you

Low tunnels can be used to protect crops early or later in the year.

intend to pick later in the year, with specially-made tunnels or a covering of horticultural fleece. Sheets of this material can either be laid directly over the plants or attached to a series of hoops to make a low tunnel or cloche. In spring, use sheets of fine mesh to safeguard plants against cabbage root fly, carrot fly, whitefly, aphids and other pests. Plants that are a target for birds can also be protected with netting.

Weeding in the vegetable garden

Whether you grow vegetables in the soil or in pots it's inevitable that you will have to deal with weeds. Apart from looking unsightly, weeds will suck up moisture and nutrients, stealing them from the vegetables you had intended to fortify. Let weeds get out of hand and they can check the growth of your vegetables by muscling in on their space, or preventing much-needed light from reaching them. They can also make picking or harvesting crops more of a chore and, depending on how out of control they get, you may not even notice when your plants are ready and waiting to be harvested.

Remove weeds that appear in vegetable beds by hand; if only a few annual weeds appear, simply tug them out before they have the chance to flower, set seed and spread like crazy through the rest of the bed. Larger populations that appear in the rows between vegetables are best removed with a hoe, which should chop through them quickly and effectively. As long as they haven't set seed, the decapitated weeds can be left on the surface to dry up naturally in the sun.

You'll never be able to completely stop all weeds from popping up, as their seeds are drawn like magnets to bare

Hoe weeds regularly to prevent competition to vegetables.

soil, but you can reduce the area they can grow in by using a variety of methods. For instance, if you plant sweetcorn in spring there will be some large gaps among the plants until they start to grow with more gusto in the summer. Try filling these gaps with short-lived vegetables, such as lettuce, which will give you an extra crop and give weeds less space to populate. Alternatively, mulch the soil around plants to prevent weeds from getting a foothold.

If you have a large area of bare soil, such as an unused patch on the allotment, cover it with plastic, landscape material, or even an old carpet, to prevent weeds from ever germinating.

Looking after crops in pots

Vegetables in containers are generally easy to look after, but you will need to give them some attention during the growing season. Anything grown this way tends to dry out more rapidly than it would if it were grown in the ground, so you will need to keep a close eye on the compost and make sure that it is kept damp. In the summer this may mean watering once or even twice a day, depending on the crop and how demanding of moisture it is. You also need to feed it regularly with the correct fertilizer.

When plants are confined they tend to grow rapidly and will soon fill the pot. At this point it is difficult to keep the plant moist enough. The foliage may start to wilt, even a few hours after it has been watered, or you may notice the plant is losing vigour. To prevent this happening, re-pot the plant into a slightly larger container (it may be necessary to do this several times during the growing season). If you notice that the roots are congested as you remove the old pot, tease them out gently or the plant will fail to anchor itself in the new container.

Harvesting

Harvesting your vegetables is exciting – after all, it's the reason you've been nurturing and tending to them for weeks or months. For the best taste, you need to pick when the crop is ripe or when it is small and tender, not when it's underipe, overripe, or left so long that it has become stringy.

With many crops it will be obvious when you need to harvest based on your experience of buying and handling vegetables in the shops. For instance, everybody is familiar with a ripe tomato, but some other plants may be less obvious, especially those that are concealed beneath the soil or hidden behind a cover of leaves.

Perhaps the hardest vegetable to decide when to harvest is the potato. As a rule of thumb, lift early potatoes when they are flowering, but maincrops can be left in the ground longer. To avoid damage to the crop, dig about 30cm (12in) away from the stem with a fork and check a few spuds first to see if they are ready before digging up the whole row.

Tug up beetroots when they have reached about 5cm (2in) in diameter, by holding the stem and pulling gently. Picks beans regularly or they'll become tough and stringy. If left courgettes can become as big as marrows, so pick them when they are young – the size depends on the variety and will be clearly stated on the seed packets. Test sweetcorn cobs when the tassels turn brown. Pull back the leaves and prick a few kernels with your fingernail. If milky sap flows out, hold and twist off.

Some vegetables can be picked by hand, but those with tough stems that connect them to the plant, such as courgettes, peppers and aubergines, will need removing with secateurs. Use scissors to harvest leafy crops cleanly.

Storing your crops

If you have a small garden it's likely that you will eat everything when you pick it, but those with more substantial vegetable gardens can often produce enough to provide food at leaner times of the year.

While sweetcorn, peas and runner beans are ideal for freezing, you may wish to pickle some of your harvest or turn crops into preserves – a glut of beans is perfect for chutney, as are any green tomatoes left at the end of their growing season. Borlotti beans can be stored by leaving the pods to dry completely and then squirreling away the beans in airtight containers.

Some vegetables can also be stored fresh. For instance, after lifting maincrop potatoes in September, leave the tubers to dry on the soil for a few hours and then place them carefully into paper sacks. Fold the top over to exclude light or the potatoes will sprout prematurely. Then store the sack in a cool, frost-free place for use until spring.

Carrots can be stored in the wooden trays used to pack fruit (you'll often see these discarded at the end of a market and you should be able to help yourself to them). Add a

Harvest ripe aubergine by cutting tough stems with secateurs.

layer of damp, but not wet, sand to trays then lay the carrots on top, ensuring they are not touching, and cover over with another layer of sand. The roots should last until March.

Cabbages can stored in net bags, suspended above the ground, for use until spring, while onions can be kept in the legs of a pair of old tights until late spring, which will allow air to reach them and prevent them getting damp.

Most vegetables are best stored in a place that doesn't get too warm and is frost-free. A shed or garage is ideal. Check crops regularly to ensure they remain healthy and discard any that show signs of disease, as this can quickly spread through the other crops in the store.

The cool conditions of a shed make the ideal place to store many vegetables.

Index

Published in 2010 by BBC Books, an imprint of Ebury Publishing.
A Random House Group Company

Copyright © Woodlands Books Ltd 2010
Words by Martyn Cox
All photographs © *Gardeners' World* magazine/BBC Worldwide 2010

The Random House Group Limited Reg. No. 954009

Addresses for companies within the Random House Group can be found at
www.randomhouse.co.uk

A CIP catalogue record for this book is available from the British Library.

ISBN 978 1 846 07920 7

Penguin Random House is committed to a sustainable future for our business, our readers and our planet. This book is made from Forest Stewardship Council® certified paper.

MIX
Paper from
responsible sources
FSC
www.fsc.org
FSC® C018179

Commissioning editor: Lorna Russell
Project editor: Joe Cottington
Copy editor: Helena Caldon
Designer: Kathryn Gammon
Picture researcher: Mel Watson
Production: Lucy Harrison

Colour origination by: Dot Gradations Ltd
Printed and bound in China by Toppan Leefung Printing Ltd

To buy books by your favourite authors and register for offers, visit www.rbooks.co.uk

---

Picture credits

BBC Books and *Gardeners' World* magazine would like to thank the following for providing photographs. While every effort has been made to trace and acknowledge all photographers, we should like to apologize should there be any errors or omissions.

Peter Anderson p79; Mark Bolton p59; Jonathan Buckley p119; Torie Chugg p191 (left); Sarah Cuttle p85 (left), p90, p94, p102 (right), p182 (right); Paul Debois p51, 52 (left), 66 (all), 67 (all); Stephen Hamilton p25 (left), p63, p115 (all), p141, p179; Sarah Heneghan p47 (right), p60 (left), p89, p166; Neil Hepworth p104, p152, p158; Caroline Hughes p13, p47 (left), p71, p108 (right), p142 (top left); Annie Hyde p44; Jason Ingram p20 (all), p31, p48, p65, p72, p82, p102 (left), p163, p192; Andrea Jones p209; Noel Murphy p85 (right); David Murray p8, p28, p52 (right); Tim Sandall p17 (all), p22, p25 (right), p27, p32 (all), p33 (all), p35, p36, p39, p41, p42, p60, p68, p80, p86 (right), p93, p97 (all), p100, p124, p129, p136 (all), p137 (all), 142 (top left and bottom), p149, p157, p174, p185, p188, p191 (right), p197, p200, p202, p206; William Shaw p15 (right), p108 (left), p132, p171 (left); Nick Smith p75, p182 (left)

Also available from BBC *Gardeners' World* magazine and BBC Books: